Scribble Scrabble

Learning to Read and Write

Success with Diverse Teachers, Children, and Families

Scribble Scrabble

Learning to Read and Write

Success with Diverse Teachers, Children, and Families

Daniel R. Meier

Teachers College
Columbia University
New York and London

This book was partially supported under the Research and Creative Scholarship and the Presidential Award for Professional Development of Probationary Faculty programs at San Francisco State University. The findings and the opinions expressed in this book do not reflect the position or policies of San Francisco State University. The work reported in this book was also assisted in part by a grant from The Spencer Foundation. The data presented, the statements made, and the views expressed are solely the responsibility of the author.

Published by Teachers College Press, 1234 Amsterdam Avenue, New York, NY 10027

Library of Congress Cataloging-in-Publication Data

Meier, Daniel R.
    Scribble scrabble—learning to read and write: Success with diverse teachers, children, and families / Daniel R. Meier.
        p.   cm.
    Includes bibliographical references and index.
    ISBN 0-8077-3883-2 (cloth : alk. paper) — ISBN 0-8077-3882-4 (pbk. : alk. paper)
        1. Language arts (Preschool)—United States—Case studies.   2. City children—Education (Preschool)—United States—Case studies.
    3. Literacy—United States—Case studies.
        I. Title: Learning to read and write.   II. Title.
    LB1140.5.L3 M45 2000
    372.6—dc21   99-048786

ISBN 0-8077-3882-4 (paper)
ISBN 0-8077-3883-2 (cloth)

Printed on acid-free paper
Manufactured in the United States of America

07 06 05 04 03 02 01 00   8 7 6 5 4 3 2 1

–For Hazelle and Kaili

Contents

Acknowledgments

Just as no book about teaching can be written without the cooperation of children, parents, and teachers, I first thank these participants for lending their words and artwork and perspectives to this book. I wish to thank all the teachers, children, and parents from the preschools in the school district in which I taught. These teachers have allowed me into their classrooms, letting me work with their children and letting me interrupt their schedules "to go read books with Mr. Meier." They have been most generous and kind with their time, their students, and their perspectives on literacy and schooling. I thank in particular Gladys, Robin, Jane, Louise, Leilani, Connie, and Ruthie for speaking with me about their literacy practices and teaching. I also wish to thank Becky, the administrator who first encouraged me to work in the district's preschools. I acknowledge, too, the parents—Bonita, Aida, Lynn, Alma, Regina, and Rochelle—who gave me valuable time from their busy lives.

There are too many children to thank by name, and so I wish to thank them all for working with me and sharing their perspectives and thoughts on literacy and schooling. They were always helpful, always willing to leave recess on the playground and come inside and read and draw and do dictation with me. They always gladly ran off to get other children off the monkey bars and off their tricycles, and held their hands as we all walked back into the school building. The children always asked for the books that I brought and listened to my favorite books and stories. I hope that I have rendered their thoughts and literacy work with sensitivity and respect.

I also wish to thank the anonymous reviewers who reviewed the initial proposal for this book. They provided me with excellent guiding points and helped steer me in fruitful directions. I especially thank Pedro Noguera, Rebecca New, Susan Britsch, Alex Casareno, Carolee Fucigna, and Violet Robinson for their supportive and encouraging responses to the manuscript. Without them, I could not have edited and changed the book into its final form. I also wish to thank two wonderful early childhood educators, Grace Angel and Norma Villazana-Price. Grace and Norma helped transcribe audiotapes and track down those always elusive references.

I thank, too, my editor at Teachers College Press, Brian Ellerbeck. Brian, with his customary sense of good humor and encouragement, carefully guided me through the proposal stage and the writing of this book. He has been a critical source of support for me as I rendered my teaching experiences onto paper. I also wish to acknowledge Karl Nyberg for shepherding the book through its production phase with great care.

Last, I wish to thank my family. My wife, Hazelle Fortich, provided me with the love and guidance to write this book. Her exhortations of "you can do it" and "keep going" were just what I needed. I also wish to acknowledge our daughter Kaili for providing me with her smile that reminded me that I was also writing this book for her. I hope, when she is older, that Kaili may just remember sitting beside me as I wrote this book.

Scribble Scrabble

Learning to Read and Write

Success with Diverse Teachers, Children, and Families

Part I

Schooling, Diversity, and Literacy Education

Bonita with daughter Akilah

Alma with son Ivan and daughter Mariella

Chapter 1

Literacy in the Preschool– Children, Teachers, and Families

"Oooh girl, you're scribble scrabbling! You oughta be ashamed of yourself!"
–Four-year-old Kyesha to Lisa, who is drawing in her journal

PURPOSE OF THE BOOK

The term "scribble scrabble" most commonly refers to children's apparently random and nonrepresentational drawings and writing. Whenever I asked the children, "What is scribble scrabble?" I always got a response.

JOHN: It's like this. (waved his hand in the air as if holding a marker and drawing random squiggles)
MARCUS: It's what babies do.
TINELLE: I don't do scribble scrabble. I make a rainbow. My mom said I can't scribble scrabble. My mom don't want me to.
ANNE: It's messy writing. The big kids [that is, four-year-olds like herself] are supposed to draw correctly.
ARTHUR: If you scribble scrabble, you might mess up your picture.
RASHEED: You got to be tall not to scribble scrabble.

In this book, I focus on scribble scrabble as a central protagonist in my attempts to find common ground between developmentally appropriate and culturally responsive literacy teaching. I intend this book for teachers, teachers-to-be, and others interested in understanding and improving the literate lives of children, teachers, and families in urban schools. The book is based on my experiences as a part-time teacher at several public preschools in the San Francisco Bay Area. Over the course of 4 years, I worked with small groups of four- and five-year-old children on enriching their language and literacy experiences. While my story focuses primarily on the literacy education of young children, I hope that readers interested in older children will be interested in hearing about critical early literacy connections for children and adults.

3

In this book, I describe those telling moments of literacy teaching and learning that reveal important intersections among development, literacy, and diversity. I draw on my teaching with the children and show the children at work and play with words and books and their life experiences. I also discuss the perspectives and expectations of teachers and parents. In doing so, I hope to broaden the scope of literacy theory and practice to make room for the voices of a more diverse group of adults. I also include relevant educational theory and research on literacy as a way to paint a broad backdrop for the literacy perspectives and actions of the children and adults. I have divided the book into three parts. In Part I, I provide important background on my role and teaching as well as relevant theoretical and pedagogical frameworks. In this first introductory chapter, I describe the context and setting of my teaching and discuss how and why I worked as a teacher researcher. In Chapter 2, I provide background on theory and practices relating to developmentally appropriate and culturally responsive literacy practices.

In Part II, Chapters 3 through 5, I describe how I taught the children and I discuss how the children's artwork, writing, and comments connect development and diversity in their literacy learning. I have tried in these middle chapters to present literacy as the children came to it rather than the other way round, and to use telling anecdotes and scenes to illustrate the most significant characteristics and themes of the children's literacy resources and interests.

In Part III, I describe and discuss the widening circles of literacy teaching and learning. In Chapters 6 and 7, I discuss ways to strengthen existing school literacy practices by including the voices and perspectives of families in their children's literacy education. In the Epilogue, I offer final reflections on the search for common ground between developmentally appropriate practice and culturally responsive teaching. To provide anonymity, I have changed the names of all children, some of the adults, all the schools, and all places.

LAYERS OF LITERACY, LAYERS OF COMMUNITY

After teaching kindergarten and first grade (Meier, 1997), I became interested in teaching preschool in my public school district. I wrote a proposal to Becky, the district's Director of Child Development, and described my plans to work with preschoolers on literacy-related activities. Becky liked my proposal and I was hired to teach on a part-time basis at one of the district's preschools. I started out teaching four- and five-year-old children at Hawthorne Preschool.

Becky suggested that I contact Carole, the head teacher at Hawthorne Preschool. I called and Carole and I agreed on a time to meet. Eager to meet Carole and get my teaching off to a good start, I brought two large cups of coffee for our meeting. I was late, though, by 10 minutes. I walked in the door at Hawthorne holding my offering of hot coffee with cream, and Carole greeted me by saying, "You're late." I felt put off and bothered, feeling that I hadn't shown enough respect to come on time. Now, 4 years later and after many conversations and shared experiences at the school, Carole's "you're late" is a distant memory. I realized that Carole's remark said to me, "This is our place of teaching and learning. We probably do some things differently than you do. We welcome you, but we have our own way of doing things here."

I also realized that Carole's greeting tells me that in the professional, personal, and social life of schools, the "ways with words" (Heath, 1983) of children and adults are interwoven with layers of community and layers of literacy. Layers of community refer to the complex network of relationships and experiences that form the basis for child and adult perspectives on the goals of schooling. Layers of literacy refer to the diversity of child and adult expectations for using literacy in and out of school. Taken together, these layers can be like the blankets covering a sleeping child, for they are familiar and comfortable traditions and practices that work well for children and adults.

The Larger Community

The public school district's child development program consists of five preschools that operate on an all-day, year-round schedule and serve children from 2.9 to 5+ years of age. The district also operates a half-day, parent–teacher cooperative nursery featuring a Spanish/English bilingual program. The city's entire preschool-age population is served by these five preschools, several Head Start preschools, and a variety of private child-care centers and preschools. Each year, the school district's preschools and the city's Head Start centers each send approximately 100 children to the district's various kindergartens. The city's private preschools also send children to the public school district and to the city's secular and parochial elementary schools.

The district's preschools currently serve approximately 400 children. With the exception of the bilingual parent nursery, the district's preschools are open year-round and serve children and families from 7:30 a.m. to 5:45 p.m. Admission to the district's early childhood centers is reserved first for residents of the city, while others apply on a space-available basis. The majority of the children are nonfee-paying due to income eligibility. As part of the stipulation by state and federal educational agencies, parents must show either proof of employment or full-time school attendance.

The children's families represent a varied cross-section of single fathers and mothers, teenage parents living with their own parents, two-parent families, grandparents and great-grandparents, all involved in raising children. In terms of the ethnic and racial composition of the children and their caretakers at all of the preschools at which I worked (not including the Spanish/English bilingual nursery), approximately 92% are African American, 3% Latino/Latina, 2% mixed Anglo/African American, 2% Anglo, 1% Asian.

The preschools are located in a city with a total population of approximately 100,000. The streets and neighborhoods where the preschool children live are located in the city's "flatlands" to the south and the west of the downtown city center, and experience a disproportionate percentage of crime and inadequate housing compared with the more affluent neighborhoods to the north and east in the city's "hill" and "foothill" communities. Historically, and somewhat paradoxically, the city also has a tradition of racial and cultural tolerance and bridge building and a commitment to promoting and strengthening its public schools.

The School Communities—Children, Families, Teachers

Over 4 years, I taught 300 children at four district preschools: Hawthorne, Bernard, Dorsey, and Casanova. The majority of my teaching occurred at Hawthorne. I conducted parent workshops at Nieva.

Hawthorne Preschool. Hawthorne is a brown wood building built on the edge of a large grass playing field. Given the lack of trees, and its open southern exposure, several of the outside walls are peeling. The preschool is located five blocks from the city's downtown center and the large university. Hawthorne serves children and families from the primarily African American and Latino neighborhoods to the south and the west.

Hawthorne has three classrooms, all on the first floor. The second story has a small room that the teachers use as a meeting room for lunch, social gatherings, and parent meetings. The back of the school has a large playground area. In the front of the playground, a large grassy area with a slight slope for rolling and running lies behind a large sandbox area. The middle of the playground consists of a set of swings, benches, a climbing structure, and a circular path that the children use as a one-way track for riding their tricycles. The kitchen is staffed by the teachers and the teaching assistants, there is no paid cook, and the food arrives by truck on a daily basis and is reheated in the kitchen. Approximately half of the children eat breakfast at the school, and all of the school's 90 children eat the school's lunch.

Breakfast is served from 7:30 a.m. to 8:45 a.m. and lunch from 11:30 a.m. to 12:00 p.m.

The largest classroom, consisting of two open spaces, adjoins the kitchen and serves the school's group of three-year-olds. The school's other two classrooms are for the four- and five-year-olds. In the classroom for three-year-olds, there are three large kidney-shaped tables for working with the children, colorful rugs, ample tubs of play toys, a kitchen and play corner, and a reading corner; the room is fronted by a long bank of windows to one side. Each child has a cubby labeled with his or her name for personal possessions. As in all the classrooms, the children's blue plastic sleeping cots are stacked up against a spare wall. The two classrooms for the older children, though smaller in size, have similar furniture, equipment, materials, toys, and resources. These two classrooms recently each acquired a computer as part of a district-wide technology grant.

Hawthorne's library is located next to the older children's classrooms. It is a small room with two windows and can hold six to eight children and one adult. The library has a sizable collection of multicultural and multilingual children's literature and nonfiction books appropriate for preschoolers. The checkout cards, with each child's name for Hawthorne's bookbag program, line one wall of the library.

Hawthorne's total of six teachers and eight teaching assistants are experienced, veteran teachers in the field of early childhood and elementary education. In terms of ethnicity, 11 teachers are African American and three are Anglo. Carole, who as head teacher also performs a supervisory role at the site, has over 30 years of experience teaching children in various settings. The majority of the teachers have spent their teaching careers in the city's child development program, and half the teachers have taught at Hawthorne for at least 10 years. The majority of the teachers live either in the neighborhoods bordering Hawthorne or in nearby cities within close driving distance. Several teachers see the preschool children's parents on a regular basis in the community and are active members of their churches.

A typical day at Hawthorne follows a set schedule, which all the teachers adhere to since the one common kitchen serves all the children's meals.

7:30 a.m.	Breakfast and activity/free choice time
9:00 a.m.	Whole group circle time
9:30 a.m.	Small group work at tables with teachers and teacher aides
10:30 a.m.	Recess
11:00 a.m.	Whole group story time
11:30 a.m.	Lunch
12:00 p.m.	Nap time
2:00 p.m.	Activity/free choice time

3:00 p.m.   Snack
3:15 p.m.   Recess
4:00 p.m.   Activity/free choice time and final pick-up

The schedule is similar at Bernard, Dorsey, and Casanova, the other three preschools where I taught.

At all of the district's preschools, there is no official parent–teacher conference day or report card of student progress. The district's child development program has an annual open house for parents in the fall, and individual preschools sponsor their own events for children and parents during the course of the year. There are no contract-guaranteed days for teacher inservice, although the child development program sponsors and funds individual and small groups of teachers to attend workshops. On occasion, the preschool teachers join the district's elementary teachers on curriculum projects. For instance, several preschool classrooms currently are involved in the district's technology grant.

The preschools hire additional specialist teachers on a part-time basis. At Hawthorne, a speech and language specialist works with small groups of three-, four-, and five-year-old children in need of extra help with language development. Hawthorne also employs a part-time dance teacher and music teacher. These two teachers work with the children once a week, teaching each class for approximately 40 minutes. Students from the continuation high school across the street also visit Hawthorne to read and play with the preschoolers. Trained by one of their high school teachers, the high school students read books to small groups of the preschoolers. After their reading sessions, the high school students help the children ride their tricycles, shoot baskets, and play football on the yard.

Over the years, the curriculum at Hawthorne has been created largely by the veteran faculty. In terms of literacy education, the teachers stress the importance of early exposure and involvement in a range of oral and written language activities. These activities include daily story time, storytelling, weekly sharing time, independent and free choice reading in the book corner, participation in a weekly bookbag reading program, multimedia CD-ROM stories and language arts games on the computer, call and response language games, songs and rhymes and finger plays, painting and drawing, special projects for holidays and other occasions, workbook-like sheets on handwriting and letter and numeral writing, oral questioning and recitation of children's names and addresses, identification of letter names and colors and numbers, and language arts puzzles and games.

Nieva, Bernard, Dorsey, Casanova Preschools. These other preschools espouse a slightly different philosophy and curriculum. Casanova and Dorsey both feature a curriculum based on Montessori philosophy and practices (Montessori, 1995). These two centers are equipped with Montessori materials—counting beads, rods, small trays and manipulatives, and beakers and containers for liquids—and the teachers and teaching assistants at these preschools have received inservice Montessori training.

Nieva is the district's only parent nursery and only Spanish/English bilingual program. Approximately two-thirds of the children are native Spanish speakers. At Nieva, three-year-olds attend from 8:30 a.m. until 11:30 a.m., and four- and five-year-olds attend from 12:30 p.m. to 3:30 p.m. Nieva is located on the same site as the Bernard preschool, which operates on the same all-day, year-round schedule as Hawthorne. A small number of the children who attend Nieva in the morning also attend Bernard in the afternoon, experiencing both a Spanish/English bilingual program and a "regular" preschool program in the same day. Both Bernard and Nieva are located in a working-class, Latino and African American neighborhood on the western edge of the city.

Casanova preschool serves two mixed-age classrooms of three-, four-, and five-year-olds. The preschool rooms are part of a larger kindergarten through grade five elementary school, which has a Spanish language immersion strand starting in kindergarten through grade five. Approximately one-fourth of the students at Casanova preschool are native Spanish speakers, and one teaching assistant in each classroom speaks Spanish.

How I Organized My Literacy Teaching

I taught the children in small groups to maximize one-to-one interaction and focus on children's individual needs and talents. I established a predictable small group format and structure, which I altered and changed as I saw fit. I worked with each group of children for about 30 minutes on a variety of language and literacy activities. Spending a morning or afternoon at a preschool site, I rotated all the older four- and five-year-old children through the activities that I had planned for the day.

During each small group literacy session, I started with an opening routine. Sitting in a circle, the children and I chanted and clapped each child's name. The children always delighted in hearing their names repeated in rhythmic unison. We then sang songs or did finger rhymes. I used this opening routine to gain a quick sense of small group community and provide a language warm-up. On occasion, I also devoted 5 minutes to sound–symbol literacy skills. I bought a pack of alphabet flash cards at a local variety store and showed the cards one at a time to the group of children. I also used a large set of animal pictures with the animal names written alongside the corresponding initial letter. In showing these alphabet cards and pictures, I alternated between saying, "A is for _____," and pointing to the object or animal and saying, "This is a

_____, and it starts with the letter A." Since some children were more familiar with the letters than others, I gave equal emphasis to the objects as to the letters.

In the second part of our session, I read two to three children's literature books with the children. I read such books as *The Very Quiet Cricket* (Carle, 1990), *The Little Red Hen* (Zemach, 1983), and *Clean Up Your Room, Harvey Moon!* (Cummings, 1991), which the children loved hearing over and over again. I also included a variety of multicultural books that spoke to the children's experiences and promoted a positive sense of cultural identity. These included such books as *Jonathan and His Mommy* (Smalls, 1992), *One Hot Summer Day* (Crews, 1995), and *Pretty Brown Face* (Pinkney & Pinkney, 1997). I also used books in different languages, like *Table, Chair, Bear* (Feder, 1995), *Moon Rope/Un lazo a la luna* (Ehlert, 1992), and *¡Salta, ranita, salta!* (Kalan, 1981). In addition, to broaden further the children's interests and literary background, I read science books such as *Reptiles* (Matero, 1994) and *Snowballs* (Ehlert, 1995), wordless books like *The Apple Bird* (Wildsmith, 1983), books about literacy and numeracy skills such as *The Calypso Alphabet* (Aagard, 1989) and *Ten, Nine, Eight* (Bang, 1983), concept books like *Understanding Opposites* (1996), chapter books like *Frog and Toad Are Friends* (Lobel, 1970), books from and about other countries like *Anansi the Spider* (McDermott, 1972), and flap books like *Spot Pasea Por el Bosque* (Hill, 1993).

I continually brought in new books for the children and at the same time returned to "old" books that the children loved. As I read, I encouraged the children to use gestures and oral language to respond to the books and stories. For example, in reading *The Little Red Hen* (Zemach, 1983), I asked the children to do the hand and body motions for planting, watering, and cutting the wheat. On other occasions, I encouraged the children to join in on certain refrains and phrases. This worked well in a book like *Chicka Chicka Boom Boom* (Martin & Archambault, 1989), which has a swinging, repetitive text easily repeated by young children. On other occasions, I encouraged the children to talk and make comments during the book reading. This worked especially well when I asked the children to pay attention to a certain aspect of the story before I started reading. For instance, before reading *Ten, Nine, Eight* (Bang, 1983), I told the children, "Pay attention to the movement of the cat and see where she goes." Since I gave the children something to look and watch for, they spontaneously chimed in as I read, "Oh, there go the cat," and "She moving to the window." I also encouraged the children to comment spontaneously on a character or story plot. For instance, in reading *Clean Up Your Room, Harvey Moon!* (Cummings, 1991), the children invariably shouted out, "His room messy!" or "There's his skates!" or "Look at the bubble gum!"

The third part of our session involved the children drawing and writing on their own. I created a journal for each child made of blank xerox paper and brightly colored construction paper. I cut out a diversity of animals, objects, and people from magazines for the children to choose and glue on their journal cover. They enjoyed picking out their own images and decorating their journals in a personal way. As they worked in their journals, I encouraged the children to draw and write as they pleased. The children worked around the one table in the library, sharing markers and pencils and talking and socializing. From time to time, I framed the children's drawing and dictation to focus on an element or theme from the books we read or on other relevant topics. I frequently took the children's oral language dictation, asking the children, "What do you want to dictate?" or "What did you draw?" Over time, as they learned my mini-routine for dictation, the children spontaneously dictated without my prompting. We often then "read" the dictation back together after I wrote.

The fourth step of small group teaching involved children's book browsing and sharing with each other. Sometimes, the children asked for books that I had just read, which happened most frequently with an exciting new book or a book with puppets and other props. The children loved to re-enact the story using the props just as I had done. I also previewed certain books by saying, "This is a book that we haven't read in a long time, but I'm sure you'll enjoy reading it again," or "This is another new book. It's got all these flaps and you lift each one up and look to see what's inside." If I wanted the children to explore the books on their own, I simply spread the books out on the floor like a reading buffet.

FROM TEACHING TO WRITING—
A PROCESS OF REINTERPRETATION

I have written this account of literacy teaching based on my experiences of literacy with the children and on my discussions with teachers and parents. In rendering these experiences and perspectives in this book, I have included educational theory and practice as a helpful conceptual frame for finding common ground between developmentally appropriate and culturally responsive literacy education.

Observing and Documenting Children's Literacy Involvement

I use two different but related perspectives for my portrait of children's language and literacy use. First, I relied on ideas associated with qualitative research (Bogdan & Biklen, 1998; Erickson, 1986; Genishi, 1982;

Goodwin & Goodwin, 1996). This collection of research strategies helped me focus on the details and qualities of the children's literacy engagement and reminded me to look for the small and daily examples of literacy growth and understanding. Second, I relied on ideas associated with teacher research and practitioner inquiry (Ashton-Warner, 1963; Bissex & Bullock, 1987; Cochran-Smith & Lytle, 1993; Goswami & Stillman, 1987; Paley, 1981). This set of notions and methods helped me connect my data collection with my own teaching and with the children's literacy learning.

In relying on elements of both qualitative and teacher research, I collected a variety of information on the children's literacy learning: spontaneous responses to books, independent book-browsing selections, book discussions, drawings and artwork, writing and dictation, and storytelling and art. I audiotaped a select number of our literacy sessions, and the children loved to hear me play back their voices. With the help of an assistant, we transcribed most of the audiotapes. I collected the children's art and literacy work, and stored items in folders according to preschool and year.

In reviewing the transcripts, my notes, and the children's literacy-related work, I looked for the most relevant details and patterns of appropriate and responsive teaching. In particular, I looked for evidence of developmentally appropriate practice, cultural and linguistic diversity, scribble scrabble, family connections, contemporary childhood, literacy as action/power/physical, common ground, and the preschool to kindergarten connection. I based Chapters 3 through 5 on these areas of literacy education.

Documenting Teacher Perspectives on Literacy

I observed the teachers' classroom strategies and informally interviewed several preschool and elementary school teachers regarding their perspectives on literacy education. In observing in the classrooms, I concentrated on the display of children's work, literacy materials and resources, literacy strategies and techniques, and general patterns of the children's participation. In the informal interviews, I asked questions regarding the teachers' views on developmentally appropriate practice and responsive literacy teaching for diverse learners.

1. How do you teach literacy in your classroom?
2. By the end of the school year (in preschool, kindergarten, or first grade), what do you want your children to have learned in terms of literacy?
3. What do you think of developmentally appropriate practices? How do you make connections to the diversity of children in your classroom?

4. How do you see the role of linguistic and cultural diversity in your literacy teaching?
5. What is the role of parents in children's literacy learning?
6. What is the place of literacy in connecting preschool with elementary school?

I also interviewed Becky, the district's Director of Child Development, and focused on administrative aspects of staff development, literacy curriculum, and the preschool to kindergarten connection. In reviewing my notes from the interviews, I looked for information pertaining to developmentally appropriate practice, culturally responsive teaching, common ground, personal background, professional negotiation, perspectives on parents, and preschool to kindergarten transition. I organized these ideas into the discussion of teacher perspectives in Chapter 6.

Documenting Parental Perspectives on Literacy

I collected information on parental perspectives on literacy through informal interviews, parental participation in Hawthorne's bookbag program, and the family literacy workshops that I conducted at the preschools. I looked for evidence of parental goals for preschool literacy, preparation for kindergarten, literacy and cultural and linguistic diversity, and the preschool to kindergarten transition. Recording the interviews through handwritten notes, I asked about parental views on literacy, development, and diversity.

1. What do (or did) you want your child to learn about literacy in preschool?
2. Do you want your child to learn the ABCs, letter names, and sounds? Do you want your child to write his/her name? What kinds of books do you want your child to read and experience?
3. Do you work on literacy outside of school with your child?
4. What do you want your child's kindergarten experience to be like? What do you want in terms of literacy education?
5. Is your child participating in Hawthorne's bookbag program? What do you think of the program?
6. If you could change anything about schools for your child, what would you change and why?

As I reviewed my notes, I looked for parental views and information on self-reflection, home literacy practices, involvement of siblings, parental involvement in schools, linguistic and cultural diversity, societal and in-

stitutional racism, and school reform. I organized these ideas into the discussion of parental literacy perspectives in Chapter 7.

When Kyesha told Lisa, "Oooh girl, you're scribble scrabbling! You
oughta be ashamed of yourself!" she showed me that children learn literacy
within powerful socially and culturally influenced traditions and expectations. Through teaching the children, and talking with their teachers and
parents, I saw anew the positive power of these traditions to influence the
early literacy education of young children. I also learned to see new possibilities for connecting developmentally appropriate practice and responsive literacy teaching.

Chapter 2

Development, Diversity, and Literacy–Toward Common Ground

Now I'm drawing Michael Jordan. He be bald headed.
I drew Michael Jordan. He's dunking over Shaq.
                              —Lonnie's dictation for his drawing

As Michael Jordan jumps and soars to the basket, children fly along and soar with him. His grace and his control and power are theirs. Jordan's "bald headed" image gives children an easily recognizable mark of identity that children crave as they develop their own sense of personal and cultural identity and affiliation. Drawing and dictating with me, Lonnie uses oral and written language to recreate over and over again the moving image of Michael Jordan soaring. Lonnie's dictation, as well as his other literacy work, also reveals the power of diverse linguistic repertoires to influence children's potential level of participation and interest in school literacy. And yet, what is the place of Lonnie's interests and language, and my teaching, within the frameworks of developmentally appropriate and culturally responsive teaching? Can we both claim our rightful places in these frameworks, and is there conceptual and pedagogical space for both of us to co-exist as we did at Hawthorne?

RETHINKING DEVELOPMENT

In seeking common ground between developmentally appropriate and culturally responsive literacy teaching, I do so against the backdrop of important recent attempts (see, e.g., Jipson, 1991; Lubeck, 1998; New & Mallory, 1994; Stremmel, 1997) to diversify the conceptual base of traditional Western views of child development. These and other recent proponents for conceptual change envision a more broadly conceived and inclusive vision of development, and wish to broaden the lenses through which we see who children are, what they can do, and what we expect them to do.

Our admittedly more ambitious aim is to stimulate new thinking about child development theory and research in general; and theory, research, *and prac-*

15

tice in the particular areas of early childhood education and early childhood special education. The lives of young children who represent diverse cultural or developmental experiences can serve as stark mirrors to hold up against our extant theoretical frameworks. (Mallory & New, 1994, p. 6, emphasis in original)

These proponents argue for diversifying the conceptual and research base for traditionally dominant views of child development. They are interested in finding new ways to make theories and conceptual frameworks of children's learning and development more reflective of the entire wealth of children's experiences and perspectives. This call for revision and rethinking is most strongly focused on the idea of developmentally appropriate practice as the most influential educational framework for early childhood educators.

What I *am* saying, however, is that we do not all have the same ideas. And even when we say that our classrooms are "developmentally appropriate," they do not all look the same. Thus, rather than writing down rules that we are all supposed to agree on and "standards" we are all supposed to meet, we might instead talk with one another and begin developing ways of organizing that allow us to have intense, sustained conversations about practice in context and over time. (Lubeck, 1998, p. 284, emphasis in original)

Developmentally appropriate practice, which has become the gold standard for high-quality educational programs and good teaching, is seen as too limited in its conceptual base and in its outreach to the varied experiences and lives of children and adults.

DEVELOPMENTALLY APPROPRIATE PRACTICE—CENTRAL TENETS

Developmentally appropriate practice is founded on the idea of teaching and curriculum matching and supporting children's growth in the traditional domains of cognitive, linguistic, social and emotional, and physical growth (Bloch, 1991; New, 1994). In the most popular and widespread interpretation of developmentally appropriate practice within the early childhood span (Bredekamp & Copple, 1997), seen as between birth to grade three, appropriate teaching starts where children are developmentally within the domains and promotes integrated, evolving competency within these areas.

Good teaching, then, matches or fits where children are *both* developmentally as a group—defined by age—and as individuals in their own right—defined by children's needs and interests. Children grow and learn through involvement in developmentally appropriate activities and practices that stimulate children's sense of curiosity and eagerness to play and discover. There is a special emphasis on opportunities for children to explore objects and tools in hands-on activities, and to be provided with a daily dose of child-directed free play time and opportunities to interact with peers. The verbs that move the vision of developmentally appropriate teaching along are not "master" and "control"—rather, the verbs are "explore," "activate," "inquire," "engage." The overall goal is for teachers to create a classroom environment and teaching curriculum that stimulate children's sense of self-discovery and satisfaction in their own learning.

The Role of the Teacher

In developmentally appropriate practice, teachers play pivotal roles in curriculum development, classroom organization, teaching, parent–teacher relations, assessment and evaluation, and community outreach. As the center of the curriculum and teaching, teachers model and guide children in learning about themselves, each other, and their expanding worlds. Teachers are also instrumental in implementing practices that are conducive to children's developmental levels and stages of understanding and inquiry.

In order to create developmentally based classrooms, teachers need extensive training in educational theory and pedagogical practices advocating child-centered teaching. In order to "make decisions about how to teach young children, teachers must know how children develop and learn" (Bredekamp & Copple, 1997, p. 36). Most important, teachers must understand the stages and developmental milestones most powerfully articulated by Jean Piaget's (1952) developmental and constructivist theories on children's growth. This developmental foundation, though, is not to be confused with the simple matching of children's chronological ages with their ability and skill for accomplishing certain behaviors or tasks. Developmental theory goes beyond "merely information about universals, 'ages and stages'" (Bredekamp & Copple, 1997, p. 36), which do not adequately portray the richness and complexity of child learning and adult teaching.

Teachers make important decisions about curriculum and practice based on "how children learn and the interaction that occurs between learning and development" (Bredekamp & Copple, 1997, p. 38). In this way, teachers use their knowledge of the complicated interplay between development and learning to gauge and judge the most successful ways to provide "appropriate experience and coaching" to "master" skills and tasks (p. 38). As children approach activities using their varied talents and skills, teachers also need to understand the role of individual differences, "including that individual's learning styles, interests, and preferences, personality and temperament, skills and talents, challenges and difficulties" (p. 40).

Parental involvement is also critical in developmentally appropriate classrooms. Programs and projects that promote family involvement enrich children's learning and provide successful early childhood education for both children and their families. The innovative early childhood programs of Reggio Emilia, Italy (Cadwell, 1997; Edwards, Gandini, & Forman, 1998), which emphasize teachers and parents working together to document and research children's learning and growth, are powerful models for effectively involving families (New, 1999).

Given the increasing cultural diversity of children and their families in schools, teachers are encouraged to become aware of the varied cultural contexts informing children's learning. Teachers are expected to use an expanded knowledge of the "rules" and "expectations for group members that are passed on from one generation to the next" (Bredekamp & Copple, 1997, p. 41). Given this multiplicity of cultural experiences and perspectives, teachers need to recognize the role of culture and the value of a "congruence" between the "rules of home and the early childhood program" so that children are not "confused or forced to choose which culture to identify with and which to reject" (p. 43).

Active Literacy Engagement

In developmentally appropriate literacy education, literacy is a natural process in which children become engaged in meaningful and creative ways with books and literacy activities. Again, teachers play a critical role by emphasizing active and playful interaction with oral and written language through nursery rhymes, songs, finger plays, stories, puppets, and children's literature. Oral language is seen on a par with written language; oral texts also can carry a message and have meaning. Dictation, the writing down of children's words by an adult to accompany children's artwork or as a freestanding story, is an influential strategy for linking oral and written language. As I taught the children, for example, I relied heavily on dictation as a beneficial language and literacy extension for the children's innermost ideas and feelings. I also used dictation to strengthen the human relationships between myself and the children; the dictation experience offers a mini public performance for children to embellish their language as it makes its way onto the written and drawn page.

This oral language/written language process and interaction also serves as a permanent artifact of children's literary expression and creativity. To further show children's development and competence, the written language can be displayed on the wall or stored away, possibly included in a portfolio of children's art and literacy work, and retrieved again for later reflection and as reminders of children's language growth. Literacy, then, validates children as both language and symbol users and makers through activities that children are capable of accomplishing.

On the other hand, developmentally appropriate practice does not advocate literacy teaching as the direct teaching of discrete literacy skills unrelated to stories and meaningful activities (*Learning to Read and Write*, 1998).

> Children take their first critical steps toward learning to read and write very early in life. Long before they can exhibit reading and writing production skills, they begin to acquire some basic understandings of the concepts about literacy and its functions. Children learn to use symbols, combining their oral language, pictures, print, and play into a coherent mixed medium and creating and communicating meanings in a variety of ways. (p. 32)

Teachers are encouraged to embed the more formal forms and conventions of written language within rich and inviting literacy activities. Literacy, then, does things for children; it helps children express themselves, articulate their needs and ideas, and make human connections with others.

Developmentally appropriate instruction does not place a premium on children creating literacy products or mastering literacy conventions like letter recognition, sound–symbol correspondence, and writing their names. Teachers and other adults also are cautioned against pushing children into literacy too fast by designing activities beyond children's developmental grasp and level of understanding. Children also are not encouraged to dwell on busy work like worksheets of rows and rows of handwriting and objects to color, which may be within the range of some children's fine-motor and perceptual skills but are not creative or meaningful and take time away from active literacy engagement. Further, teachers are encouraged to vary student groupings, not relying on whole group instruction where children sit for long periods of time listening to adults. Center activities and small group work are emphasized as they promote ample opportunities for social interaction and talk about language and literacy.

Reconceptualizing Appropriateness

In the polar nature of the current framework, developmentally appropriate practices are contrasted with developmentally inappropriate practices. These latter goals and strategies neither enrich nor interest children, and push children too far, causing a lack of synchrony between children's developmental capabilities and the demands of the literacy activities at hand. And yet, as I worked in the preschools and as I taught, I saw and heard and used practices and perspectives that could be called developmentally inappropriate. These included worksheets of letters to trace, identification of letter names, memorization of alphabet flash cards, and children practicing writing their names.

What can be viewed as developmentally inappropriate is not entirely explained away by teachers' lack of knowledge of developmental theory and practice, and other factors such as low-quality preservice teacher training and inservice staff development, low salaries, difficult work conditions, and lack of coordination with other preschools and elementary schools. These are important and critical issues, and they influence teaching practices and the quality of instruction, and yet they do not entirely explain why some views and practices considered inappropriate have persisted and still do.

What some see as developmentally inappropriate literacy education are, in part, practices and ideas influenced by social and cultural expectations and traditions regarding language and literacy use (Bruner, 1996; Ochs, 1988; Scribner & Cole, 1981; Vygotsky, 1978, 1986). These practices and expectations also are influenced by the accumulation over time of historical and political forces of racism and structural inequality in schools (Cummins, 1986; Delpit, 1995; hooks, 1994). Efforts to reconceptualize developmentally appropriate practice, then, need to account for these social and cultural influences on language and literacy use.

CULTURE, DIVERSITY, AND LITERACY

As I spent time teaching in the preschools, I found that I needed to change my teaching to reflect some of the needs and wishes of the children, teachers, and families. What was I doing and why? I changed my teaching to include, for instance, more attention to such alphabet-related activities as alphabet flash cards and helping the children write their first names. In making these and other changes, I became more responsive to the children and to the adults in the schools. At the same time, too, I looked for ways to connect developmentally appropriate literacy practices with relevant ways to interest and engage the children.

Culturally Responsive Teaching

Culturally responsive teaching (Au & Jordan, 1981; Delpit, 1995; hooks, 1994; Ladson-Billings, 1994) speaks to the cultural and personal identities and educational aspirations of children and adults. Ideas and practices associated with this perspective point to reconceptualizing traditional purposes and pathways for academic success. Culturally responsive teaching practices work to promote greater social and cultural inclusion, improve student academic achievement, and empower parents as advocates for their children's education.

In such an "engaged pedagogy" (hooks, 1994), "critical thinking" and "student expression" are valued (p. 20), and students and teachers work along the same lines to enliven the shared curriculum, both working to see education as "the practice of freedom" (p. 21). In this process of questioning the past and the present, and seeking to "transform the curriculum" (p. 21), students and teachers work to bring about a new and different kind of social, educational, and political landscape. Essential to this challenge, teachers must know their students—know "our parents, our economic status, where we worshipped, what our homes were like, and how we were treated in the family" (p. 3). The anticipated structural and pedagogical changes in schooling as we now know it, then, come from the potential for closeness and intimacy of human interaction in classrooms.

There is a premium placed on relating to students as individuals and as members of cultural communities.

> Instead of idiosyncratic and individualistic connections with certain students, these teachers work to assure each student of his or her individual importance. Although it has been suggested that teachers unconsciously favor those students perceived to be most like themselves (or some ideal) in race, class, and values, culturally relevant teaching means consciously working to develop commonalities with all the students. (Ladson-Billings, 1994, p. 66)

In working with African American children, the central challenge is to better understand how teachers can help students "not only achieve academic success but also achieve positive identity as African Americans" (Ladson-Billings, 1994, p. 12).

In responsive teaching, children's personal and cultural identities are intimately connected. In schools, though, this bond between language and identity has not been cultivated, leaving African American and other children without a strong sense of self and a strong literary voice to express themselves (Willis, 1995). It is a challenge, then, for a young African American child to "wrestle with an internal conflict that is framed by the sociohistorical and sociocultural inequalities of U.S. society" and "come to grips with how he can express himself in a manner that is true to his 'real self,' and yet please his teacher and audience of readers who are, in effect, evaluating his culture, thinking, language, and reality" (Willis, 1995, p. 33).

In this critical process of linking identity with literary expression, teacher desire and respect for children are pivotal in helping children succeed in school. In the realm of language and literacy learning, this drive for students to excel is often more valuable than generic teaching strategies.

> Certainly, a teacher's ability to "break it down" [regarding language] would depend on how well s/he knows the students and understands their cultures. Likewise, a teacher's desire to "break it down" would depend on his/her respect for the students and their cultures; indeed, the level of respect would determine whether or not the teacher would even realize a need to "break it down." Here again, methodology is secondary to attitude. (Moore, 1998, p. 2)

Teachers' understanding of culture and their interest and respect for students go hand in hand. Skilled teachers are skilled in this perspective because they have good strategies that they implement within a culture of respect and understanding.

A related aspect of this respect building is the fostering of a sense of community in the classroom. In this way, "teachers believe that students have to care, not only about their own achievement but also about their classmates' achievement" (Ladson-Billings, 1994, p. 69). In culturally relevant teaching, activities and projects have built-in elements that encourage students working together as teachers guide and teach students in learning to work collaboratively. This encourages students to work together as partners in each other's educational achievement and promotes the view of "community-building as lifelong practice that extends beyond the classroom" (Ladson-Billings, 1994, p. 73). Teachers also are guided in this push for community by a desire not to leave any student "behind" in their classroom (Moore, 1998, p. 2). The progress of the entire class is measured by the sum total of each individual student.

A Literate Voice

As articulated in the developmental continuum underlying the perspective of developmentally appropriate practice, the children whom I taught were just beginning to grapple with the new forms and symbols of literacy in a formal school setting. As articulated in the view of culturally responsive teaching, though, the children were already experts in their desire to express their personal and cultural identities in our language and literacy activities. As I taught the preschoolers, I worked to nurture their sense of a literate voice and hoped that this would connect development, diversity, and literacy.

The use of children's literature that speaks to children's interests in the world and their cultural identities (Bishop, 1990; Harris, 1990) played a major role in this process of developing a literate voice. As I read and discussed children's literature that interested children on both developmental and responsive levels, these stories and books encouraged storytelling and oral language play (Lee, 1991). The use of literature also became a springboard for children to create and interpret books and stories according to their own ways of using language from home and community. In this melding of home and school experiences with language and literacy through a common focus on literature, the children created their own "speakerly texts" (Gates, 1988, as cited in Lee, 1991) and engaged in a Vygotskian (1986) process of connecting language, interaction, and culturally influenced discourse styles (Lee, 1991).

As children play with language in social situations, they rely on others to up the ante and consequently think and feel about language in more complex ways (Bruner, 1986, 1996; Dyson, 1993, 1997; Vygotsky, 1978, 1986). This strong bond among thought, language, and interaction has its roots in the interplay between social speech and inner speech (Vygotsky, 1978, 1986). At an important point in children's language development, socialized speech (speech for regulating one's behavior in the world and speech for others) is turned inward, and language takes on interpersonal (between people) and intrapersonal (for oneself) functions. Speech (a first-order or immediate symbol system for children) and other sign-using activities like writing (a second-order or once-removed symbol system) have both biological and sociocultural origins. As children learn and grow, they gain control over both their own biological natures and their behavior as enacted with other children and adults.

As the preschoolers talked and socialized with each other as they engaged in literacy activities, the children influenced each other's understanding of the forms and functions of literacy. What happened off the page, then, was as important as what happened on the written or drawn page (Dyson, 1997). As children are encouraged to support their own literacy learning, and that of others, these opportunities promote social cohesion and the development of a literary voice. For learners in diverse classrooms, it is important to make "curricular space" (Dyson, 1997) for children's varied linguistic and social resources and interests. These opportunities allow for verbal performances (Dyson, 1993) for children that bring their social and cultural talents and experiences to bear on school-based literacy activities. The chance for performance within the public, and the private, worlds of the classroom further encourages children to create their own genre forms. This possibility for performance enables children to create their own genres, forms, and styles with oral and written language (Dyson, 1993).

The preschoolers whom I taught experimented with literacy in order to find their own genres and voice as authors and literary participants (Bakhtin, 1981, 1986). They did so through repeated opportunities for dialogue and conversation with each other, with me, with books, and with their writing and drawing. In this way, I afforded the children literary experiences that promoted a sense of "addressivity," which is defined as "the [text] quality of turning to someone" (Bakhtin, 1986, p. 99). The activities, and the way that I structured them over time, helped put the children in a dialogical or conversational relationship (Bakhtin, 1981) with words, letters, story characters, and different kinds of books. In creating activities that mixed symbols and characters and genres, I wanted the children to experience the "heteroglossia" of language and texts (Bakhtin, 1981), which can be seen as the accumulated sound and sense of stories and books over time. In this process of the children getting to know particular books and stories, many for the first time, I also wanted the children to bring in their "intimate genres and styles" of language use to gain greater "proximity" (Bakhtin, 1986, p. 97) between their voices and the voices of our literary texts. I tried, then, to promote the perception of literary texts and stories as friends and family—close relations whom the children would like to know, converse with, and return to again and again.

TOWARD COMMON GROUND

I realize that actually implementing either of the two major perspectives on learning and literacy that I have discussed is a major undertaking. The path toward creating developmentally appropriate and responsive classrooms and literacy education is long and hard. It is not easy to do well or quickly. Yet, in teaching the preschoolers, and working with the teachers and the children's families, I discovered new possibilities for common ground in both theory and practice.

First, in teaching and interacting with the children, I tried to blend elements of developmentally appropriate and culturally responsive practices. I did so in several central ways. In an overall way, I tried to read and discuss quality children's literature, provide predictable language and interactional routines, offer opportunities for talk and social interaction, create literacy activities promoting a sense of self and cultural identity, include work on selected basic literacy skills, cultivate a literary voice for the children as individuals, and encourage the children's experimentation with varied literary genres and styles. And I worked at this over several years in order to improve my orchestration of these elements.

Second, I created opportunities for the children themselves to be both developmentally appropriate and responsive with and to each other. I did so by creating opportunities for talk and interaction around open-ended and semi-structured literacy activities. In short, the activities blended child involvement and my own structuring and guidance. For example, in working with each other in their journals, the children often helped their peers write or draw and did so with just the right amount of assistance. This happened when I suggested that a friend might help, or the children themselves asked a friend what he or she wanted help drawing or writing, and either showed or helped complete the task. In this way, the children made their own decisions regarding the developmental appropriateness of the situation at hand, and they often communicated their intentions and responses in familiar and comfortable ways.

Third, I observed and talked with the other teachers. Although I taught part-time, the other teachers included me in their professional and social lives in the schools. I became, then, part of the social and professional milieu of the schools and a partner in the other teachers' efforts to strengthen literacy education for the children and their families. I learned, too, that in watching and listening to the teachers, I gained a better sense of how and why they taught literacy. I came to see that what I (and others) might consider developmentally inappropriate was often appropriate and beneficial both to the teachers and to the children. The teachers, then, gave important added dimensions to the dominant two-dimensional picture of what constitutes developmentally appropriate curriculum for diverse children *and* adults.

Fourth, the parents and families I worked and talked with helped show me new ways of conceptualizing appropriate literacy practices and making them more sensitive to responsive teaching. The voices of the parents, articulate and poignant, also revealed to me that parents too learn in developmental and responsive ways alongside their children. The pursuit of common ground, then, must include children and their families for real changes in thinking and practice to occur.

Fifth, reflecting on and struggling with my own teaching—with my own sense of identity as a teacher—helped me see new ways to connect the frameworks. When I started teaching the children, I had lists of appropriate and inappropriate practices in the back of my mind. These lists delineated the boundaries separating successful and unsuccessful literacy instruction, and to some extent they were helpful, but they also oversimplified and demystified the art of teaching. Time after time, the children's responses to me, to each other, and to literacy proved more sophisticated and surprising than the lists of appropriate practice gave the children (and we teachers and parents) credit for. So I went back and reread ideas about responsive teaching, dialogue and addressivity, and literary voice to see the greater power and force in the children's literacy actions and words. I also went back and talked with teachers and parents, mulling over their ideas and perspectives in relation to my own practices and views. And in the end, my dual role as teacher and researcher helped—teaching *and* documenting my teaching gave me the building blocks for thinking and writing about the children's literacy education.

I recently attended a conference on the innovative Reggio Emilia approach from Italy (Cadwell, 1997; Edwards et al., 1998; New, 1994). After seeing the slides of gorgeous environments and intricate and sophisticated social collaboration and intellectual work by the young Italian children, I left feeling depressed. Why can't I and others do what the Reggio teachers do? What is stopping us from achieving such educational beauty? Then, as I walked back to my car and later on as I sat down to write, I started to see the slides and snapshots of the children I worked with at Hawthorne, Nieva, Casanova, and Dorsey. I saw children laughing and laughing as they tried to memorize *Go Away, Big Green Monster* (Emberley, 1993), sharing with passion what they liked to do with their families as we discussed *In Daddy's Arms I Am Tall: African Americans Celebrating Fathers* (Steptoe, 1997), and connecting home to school as when Julio dictated, "This is my mommy and daddy and I will love them all day if I want to."

I know that the children and I have demonstrated developmentally appropriate and culturally responsive teaching and learning capabilities. I know, also, that this can translate into successful literacy learning, positive cultural identity, and connections with others and with school. The slides of the children, then, show a mixing of developmental and responsive literacy education, as well as beautiful and artful teaching and learning. I learned, too, to see more in the moment-to-moment movement of the children's talk, texts, gestures, and drawings. I saw anew how the movement and speed of literacy with children is often lithe and quick, children moving my initial focus on a picture or word toward new and darting directions. In this way, literacy as enacted with children does not always follow a stage or step-like progression from simple to complex, from the introductory to the sophisticated, from beginning to end. Rather, the teaching–learning movement often inverts itself, as the process becomes dynamic and back-and-forth and learning, experience, and development swirl together like food colors in water.

I like the word "experience" because the children also revealed how they base their expanding knowledge of literacy on an aggregate of literacy experiences. As their teacher, I often planned and taught with the idea of the children learning new words, new ideas, new letters, new ways of oral and written language. The children went along with my plans, discussing books and sharing their thoughts and drawing pictures. And yet, from their point of view, the gems of literacy are more basic, more fundamental than I anticipated. Children get into books and reading and writing because of the tantalizing possibility for representing and changing themselves and their worlds. From their point of view, literacy moves and flies and jumps just ahead of the children. When Lonnie dictated, "Now I'm drawing Michael Jordan. He be bald headed. I drew Michael Jordan. He's dunking over Shaq," Lonnie got the past, present, and future of his literacy development all wrapped into one. As Lonnie draws, Michael soars. As Lonnie talks, Michael dunks. And although Michael was dunking and bald headed way before Lonnie drew him, the experience of drawing and dictating captures and encapsulates the essence of Michael as experienced by a four-year-old child.

Part II

Literacy, Children, and Teaching

Rochelle with her mother Kathleen, and her daughters
Jasmine, Jordanáe, and Jennifer

Regina with her son Ryen, and daughters Chatani and Brianna

Chapter 3

Physical, Action, Power–The Roots of Literacy for Young Children

Then he nibble hisself out.
> –Ashley describing how *The Very Hungry Caterpillar*
> emerged from his cocoon

How can we make literacy and the language arts central to the school lives of young children? The preschoolers have shown me that the task of creating classroom teaching practices that fit children's apparent levels or places of language arts development is a hard one. It is a challenge because children's lives and their literacy learning both are in a state of mutual flux, both are intertwined in a dialogical process (Bakhtin, 1981, 1986; Wertsch, 1980, 1991) of private/public and inner/outer language use in home, community, and school. Children are, in other words, just learning how to be and experience the world, while at the same time discovering how literary skills and tools can help affirm their identity and place with themselves, family, and friends.

Although new to much of the content and symbols of literary making and interpretation, children are not starting at the beginning of an upward climb toward the acquisition of more advanced and complicated literacy skills and strategies. Rather, and here I take a *long view* of literacy learning and language arts education, the children are already experiencing complicated and sophisticated problem-solving and expressive challenges as they read, discuss, draw, and write in preschool. In this extended view of literacy and language arts education across grade levels and classrooms, children are not solely learning the building blocks in preschool. Listening and reacting to a story, discussing it with each other, rendering a drawn picture, dictating an accompanying text, comparing authors, manipulating objects to illustrate a text, comparing notes on writing words, arguing about story plot—the children actually are beginning at what often is seen as the end. They are interested and want to struggle with literary skills and tools to make words and ideas more accessible and more relevant to them.

The roots of literacy—what I call literacy as physical, literacy as action, and literacy as power—are present in children's earliest literacy engagement and development and persist in new forms and perform new functions during children's later elementary school years and beyond. Literacy as physical refers to children's connections to the physical world through gesture and other concrete connections in literacy activities; literacy as action refers to the children's interest in the plot and movement of literary texts; literacy as power refers to the potential of literacy to strengthen children's social and cultural identities. Taken as a threesome, these roots reveal a beginning foundation both in conceptual and pedagogical terms for seeing and helping children gain a sturdy foothold in their earliest literacy learning in schools.

LITERACY AS PHYSICAL

I read *Happy Birthday, Moon* (Asch, 1982) to the children. The book tells a story about a bear who wants to buy a birthday present for the moon. After I read the story, the children and I discussed the book. At one point, I asked the children, "Can the moon have a birthday?" John excitedly replied, "No! He don't got no eyes!" John was right; the moon depicted in the book had no eyes or other facial features.

On another occasion, LaShonda and Byron were drawing and writing in their journals. LaShonda, watching Byron draw, asked him, "You makin your hand?" Byron replied, "Yeah" (as he continued to trace his hand with a marker). LaShonda took a marker and helped him. "This is how you make your nails." Byron looked pleased at the addition to his drawn hand.

In a third situation, Anthony and Katima also were drawing in their journals. Katima looked over at Anthony's drawing of a "boy dinosaur" and said, "What are you gonna do now?" Anthony replied matter-of-factly, "I just have to put all this inside of him so he can have some meat. He got a lot of stuff in his tummy."

"He don't got no eyes!" "You makin your hand?" "I just got to put all this stuff inside him." These three snippets of literacy, as well as others from our literacy work, show how the children liked to connect the physical aspects of their worlds with their emerging talents to render their experiences and ideas through drawing and writing. In these instances, the children tried to link concrete physical experiences with thought and language (Vygotsky, 1978, 1986). The children relied on their familiar knowledge of the gestural and physical aspects of their worlds in order to discover the new potential of literacy tools and images. In terms of teaching practice, this interest in the physical world links the preschool children *back* to their experiences as infants through the continued movements of their hands and bodies and voices for communication and exploration. In terms of theoretical ideas about children's literacy learning, this interest forms an important line of development and responsiveness to the world and people as children translate earlier skills and talents into new forms of literacy representation.

In order to combine the practical and the theoretical here, I looked for ways that literacy activities could build on the children's propensity for using gesture and other ways of connecting literacy with the physical world. I also thought about linking physical and concrete experiences with the idea of a zone of proximal development for literacy (Vygotsky, 1978, 1986), which can be defined as the developmental space between what children can do alone and what they can do with the expert assistance of others. I learned that relying on gesture and concrete experiences serves as a home base for adventurous forays into the world of school literacy. This emphasis on the physical world—from "He don't got no eyes," to "I just got to put all this stuff inside him"—gives children a useful and valuable starting place for experimenting with and learning about visual signs and symbols in their literacy learning (Britton, 1983; Vygotsky, 1978, 1986).

> This history [of children's written language] begins with the appearance of the gesture as a visual sign for the child. The gesture is the initial sign that contains the child's future writing as an acorn contains the future oak. Gestures, it has been correctly said, are writing in air, and written signs frequently are simply gestures that have been fixed. (Vygotsky, 1978, p. 107)

Further, the use of gesture and links to the concrete physical world also are related to children's play, make-believe, and narrative (Britton, 1983).

> I am inclined to believe that in the early stages the distinction between so-cially determined reality and the story world is essentially a distinction be-tween two orders of meaning, those derived from first-hand experience, and those *assigned* for the purposes of make-believe play and fictional stories. (p. 9, emphasis in original)

In this process, children's grounding of literacy in concrete and physical experiences with the world is an important initial move toward learning to use abstract literary symbols and signs.

The power of gesture and physical movements of a marker or the placing of a finger can direct literary action and plot and the immediate social human interaction with others. In reading *Ten, Nine, Eight* (Bang, 1983), I asked the children to keep an eye on the cat as the only animal who appears, disappears, and then reappears in different places in the illustrations. I did so because I knew that this emphasis on the concrete movement of the animals in the book would capture the children's attention and draw them into the book. At one point as I pointed to a page, I said to the children, "All of the animals except the cat don't move. How does the cat move?" Given the premium that I, like many other teachers, place on using language itself to interpret the language of book texts and illustrations, I expected a verbal response to my verbal query. Aamal, though, didn't see it this way. "Like this," Aamal said as he got down on the floor and made the wordless movement of a cat. I laughed. "Yes, you're right," I said. "That's how the cat moved." Although I expected a verbal response, Aamal's gesture and concrete cat-like movements answered my question perfectly; he had a concrete connection both to the action of the book and to the context in his mind (Cazden, 1982) of what cats do in the real world. Playing at the cat, essentially making believe for a few moments that *he* was the cat, allowed Aamal to get into the story (literally) and to show his literary understanding. If I had told him to stay in his seat and verbally express a response, this would have limited Aamal from drawing on his knowledge of the experienced world (and therefore not allowed him to be responsive to my question) *and* would have curtailed his inclination to act out his answer to my question (thus not allowing him the developmental space for answering my question).

When I read *We're Going on a Bear Hunt* (Rosen & Oxenbury, 1989) with the children, I showed them the gestures that accompanied the action of the book. When the characters in the book lifted their legs to cross the cold river, so did we. When they walked through the mud, we pretended to take off our shoes and lift our feet across the sticky mud. In using these gestures to accompany the physical world of the book, the children also played at a pretend world—they suspended their belief that they were actually in a classroom, and simultaneously made believe that they were in the river and in the mud.

After reading the entire book I turned to the inside of the back cover, which shows the bear walking along the seashore with his back turned. Normally, when I reach the inside of the back cover, I say to the children with great sadness, "Nothing to read." At the sight of the forlorn bear, though, I asked the children, "Where is the bear going? Why does he look sad?"

TATYSHA: He wanted to eat people.
CLAUDE: He was sad 'cuz the people won't let him in the house; he
        wanted to eat the people.
NICHOLAS: He want them people.
NEEMA: He was walkin' home. He was knocking on the door.
SHATANI: He was scared.
KATIMA: He mad.
ASWANA: He was crying.

ANTHONY: The bear was crying because he couldn't get into the house.
  They closed the door and locked it. Your turn. (pointing to Eva)
EVA: He was sad because he didn't get anything and he wanted to lie
  down.
TAWANDA: He likes to eat, that's why he's sad.

The children were quite interested in an illustration after the official end
of the story. The picture of the forlorn bear most likely caught their interest because of the mix of the bear's slow physical movement and apparent
sadness. The children wanted to respond to my questions because the very
physical and concrete depiction of the bear along the seashore spoke to their
developmental attachment to the physical world; the movement of the bear
walking away told and signaled something of importance to the children.
At their age and experience with the world, they are keen to see and learn
how movement and emotion can be connected in human (and bear) relations. Accustomed to discussing books as based on their own experiences
and thoughts as a small group, the children also responded to my questions in responsive ways. They built on and incorporated elements of each
other's comments—they liked the rhythm of starting their comment with
the alliterative "he," and initially liked the idea of the bear eating and then
switched more to his emotions of being "scared" and "sad." Grounded in
a literary question that focused on the power of the bear's physical and
concrete movements, this activity helped the children's sense of development and responsiveness to work in tandem.

On another occasion, I read *Snowballs* (Ehlert, 1995), which is a colorful book about snow animals made out of various kinds of textiles and
common objects in the environment like bottle caps and raisins. I pointed
to the bird seed in the first few pages and asked the children what it was.
"My grandma got one of those things [bird feeder] and she put it outside,"
Lavon said. Although he didn't name the correct term of bird seed, Lavon
had the idea of the function of the bird feeder and the familial connection
with his grandmother. His response indicates his developmental place in
answering verbally ("one of those things") and his responsive place in
answering with reference to family and his physical world ("my grandmother" and "she put it outside").

In the first half of the book, I pointed to all the interesting objects and
asked the children what they were. I discovered that when the children
did not know the name of the actual object, they commented on its function or place in the larger depiction of a snow person or snow animal. For
instance, in the illustration of a snow dad, I asked the children about the
nine corn kernels that form the snow dad's mouth. The children didn't
know what they were, but all said, "Mouth!" When I asked about the snow

dad's nose, they were all able to say, "Strawberry!" In the illustration of a "cool snow boy," I asked the children about the two bolts that form the eyes. The children said, "Eyes!" I then told them that the eyes were made of bolts. I asked them about the two ears. "Wheels!" the children replied. If I had insisted that the children identify the objects rather than the facial features, a number of children would have been left out. If I had persisted in this way, I would have put a premium on children identifying objects that they all couldn't identify *through language*. By expanding my questions, I broadened the possible responses and gave the children more developmental flexibility for responding.

In the second half of the book, the snow people and snow animals start to melt. I asked the children for their thoughts on why the snow people melted.

LAVON: The bird ate the snow.
LIZA: The squirrel ate the snow.
MARVIN: The sun's white and the snow is white.

Again, the children's comments indicate their connection to the physical world and their interest in explaining how concrete experiences work. Marvin's explanation, "The sun's white and the snow is white," for example, shows the children's talent to use the language of their experienced world to make sense of literacy.

In reading a big-book version of *Quick as a Cricket* (Wood, 1982), a sophisticated book about playing with language and similes, the children and I played with the idea of filling in the phrases, "as quick as a _____," or "as slow as a _____." At one point, after I read a page with an illustration of a bee, Joseph suddenly remarked, "I saw one bad bee and he stinged someone." To which Jeremiah immediately asked, "What color stripes he had on?" Joseph and Jeremiah, as the other children listened with interest, then discussed the particulars of this bee sighting. They obviously enjoyed focusing on children's very concrete and physical interest in bees—bees buzz and bees sting. And along the way, by adding the new protagonist of "one bad bee," which spurred on Jeremiah's wondering if he actually knew the particular bee by its "stripes," Jeremiah and Joseph increased all of the children's (and my) interest in the book. For Joseph and Jeremiah, the content of literacy and its immediate associations (such as "one bad bee") are not to be separated from the sociocultural impetus of classroom life for children. Bees in a book are interesting to discuss with your friends because they're bees and they almost always make for a good story that almost all children (and most adults) can relate to.

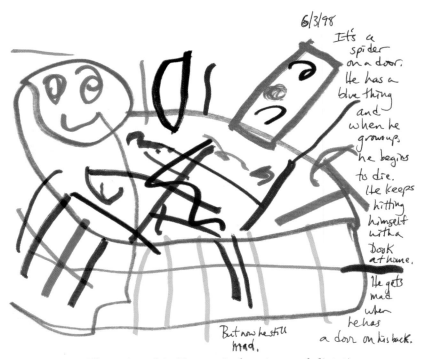

6/3/98

It's a spider on a door. He has a blue thing and when he grows up, he begins to die. He keeps hitting himself with a book at home.

He gets mad when he has a door on his back.

But now he still mad.

Plates 1 and 2. Tammy's drawing and dictation

black wing

orange thing - sting her on her finger

red spider

big thing of pie

purple big spider without no eyes, his blind

blue paint Coke pot her face thing

int the pot

4/29/98

water blue

fell into this green stuff.

Plate 3. Rodney—"A Dragon!"

Plate 4. Rodney—"Dragon Rex"

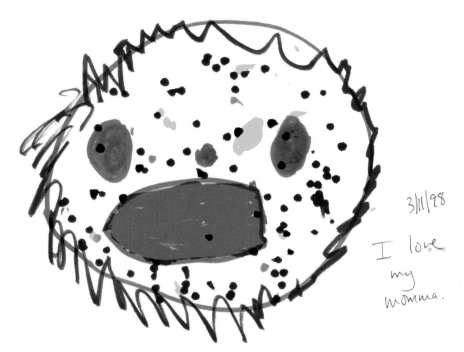

Plate 5. Liza's drawing and dictation

Plate 6. Ashayah's drawing and dictation

Plate 7. LaTasha's drawing, writing, and dictation

Plate 8. Arthur's family watercolor

Their little discussion of the "one bad bee" not only made the book a more familiar and concrete literary experience for the children, but gave an added layer of narrative and experience to our reading. By enlivening the story and engaging the children (and me), Joseph and Jeremiah point the way to what's developmentally and culturally responsive *of the moment*; as the small group format allows for extended conversation, the children's out-of-school experiences and interests (in "one bad bee" and others) spontaneously enrich and strengthen the readings of our literary texts.

This kind of dynamic process also promotes extended moments of addressivity (Bakhtin, 1986), in which the children can experience and practice using their linguistic and literacy talents for moving closer to each other as both literary participants and co-participants in the world of school literacy. As a teacher, this is what I want. I want the children to turn to the book that I'm reading, listen to and take in its content, form, and language. I also want this teacher-to-book-to-child thread of teaching to be strengthened and enriched as a shared literary experience. When the children turn to each other (and to me as adult) because of their interest in sharing their life experiences ("I saw one bad bee and he stinged someone"), they are making their own connections to a book. It is in this turning to books and words and ideas via other children and adults that encourages children to interpret and reinterpret what I am reading and discussing. Given the opportunity to connect their knowledge of the physical world with literacy, the children enjoy building on and embellishing experience through language ("What color stripes he had on?") in response to each other. This is the kind of *I'll-put-in-and-then-you-add-on* strategy that encourages children to self-scaffold literacy content through the experiential knowledge of their own lives.

Where does this strategy come from? From my work with the children, I see its origin in the incremental steps that children like to take as they learn new ways of crossing boundaries between their known experiential worlds and the more unfamiliar worlds of school literacy. Later on the same morning of the bee exchange, Jeremiah and Joseph looked at *Quick as a Cricket* by themselves. Each holding the book with one hand, they used their other hand to point and gesture to the book's characters. "OK," Joseph said, "I'll be the shark and you be the boy." Joseph uses the gesture of pointing to command *social attention* from Jeremiah, and their joint use of gesture physically links the boys with what they see in the book. Again, the children use the *I'll-put-in-and-then-you-add-on* strategy that makes sense as developmentally and culturally engaged instruction because of its potential for encouraging the children "to break down" (Moore, 1998) books and language into their essential parts and ideas.

Joseph and Jeremiah then looked at a big book of dinosaurs and again pointed at an illustration of several dinosaurs on a double-page spread.

JOSEPH: I'm him! I'm him! I'm him!
JEREMIAH: You can't be three of them!
SHATANI: (selecting another big book on dinosaurs and sitting down with Ashari on the rug, right next to Joseph and Jeremiah) I'm long neck [diplodocus]. He's eating. Long necks do eat trees. (now turning to the boys and pointing to the book) Look. We got the long neck, too.

The children's pointing gestures at the dinosaurs provide an immediate *way in* to literacy, a concrete connection with the characters that enable the four children to make an immediate connection with the books and with each other. Physically tapping on and pointing to the book's page and proclaiming, "I'm him! I'm him!" and "Look. We got the long neck, too," the children increase the degree of addressivity toward the book and toward each other. In this simultaneous turning toward the book's characters and each other, all four children effectively give themselves a way into the book and also frame the reading as a shared, communal activity.

The physical world and the role of gesture are also important in the children's drawing and written language exploration. Rosa, a Spanish speaker who made steady progress in her English language development during her 2 years in preschool, loved to draw and talk about her family members. For Rosa, as for the other English language learners in the preschools with whom I worked, the opportunity to draw and then dictate using oral language *as the children pointed* to their drawings proved a beneficial process. It offered the children an opportunity to make the most of what they knew of English (Fillmore, 1979) and to use these opportunities over and over again for increased practice and fluency.

Rosa drew her family members and friends in her journal, as depicted in Figure 3.1. "My mom, my daddy, my friend, my other friend/mi otra amiga, baby, my grandma/mi abuelita." Here and in other instances, Rosa gains experience in one-to-one correspondence of affixing oral language to each drawn picture, thereby gaining a beginning sense of an oral language–written language connection that will help lay the foundation for later sound–symbol correspondence in learning how to read and write on her own. Rosa also uses gesture to point to her drawings and claim them as her own within the public space of working with the other children. Like waving a magic wand and saying special words, Rosa points and brings her drawings to life through gesture and language. And this is more than simple labeling. Rosa's words eventually group the separate figures to-

FIGURE 3.1. Rosa's Drawing and Dictation

my mom
mi mama

my daddy

my friend

my
grandma
mi
abuelita

my other friend
mi otra amiga

baby

6/4/97

gether, creating her family and giving shape and content to her drawings through language.

During another journal session, I watched Leonard gingerly hold a fistful of markers above the blank sheet of paper. Then, drawing orange marks on the left and black lines on the right, Leonard added a purple squiggle in the middle. I asked Leonard "to tell me about your picture or anything else you want." Leonard, who received speech and language services from a specialist teacher at the school, often did not want to do dictation or had a difficult time doing it, and so he often liked to nod in agreement if I suggested a short written text to accompany his drawings.

Leonard moved his finger in quick, darting squiggles around the page without saying anything. I was perplexed at first, but as I noticed how Leonard continued to move his finger in squiggle gestures, I caught on and drew the little marks for him to represent his movements; his squiggle gestures did the talking. After eight or nine squiggles, he put his index finger on the page and then moved it straight up into the air. "Like this," he said finally, "like a bird." He did the straight-up gesture once again, this time pinching his thumb and index finger together as if lifting up a long thin piece of string. I caught on just in time, and I made a small dot for him on the page to indicate the taking off point for Leonard's "bird."

On another occasion, Leonard started to draw his own version of the small squiggles. Then toward the close of his drawing, he made a small dot like the one I made to indicate the bird. "I made it high," Leonard said as he moved his fingers up into the air from the dot. Using his fingers as a once-removed gesture, Leonard connected the physical and the drawn, the representational and the symbolic, with the movement of a bird from his daily life experiences. It was as if Leonard were making a real line up from the paper and creating a three-dimensional piece of art.

For Leonard, gestures and connections to the concrete physical world greatly helped express and depict the content and meaning of his literacy. The use of gesture enabled Leonard to turn the two-dimensional task of drawing and writing into a more real-life and familiar three-dimensional physical experience. His gestures of lifting his hand up into the air to indicate the flight of the bird also indicate how some children, playing at the boundaries of first- and second-order symbol systems (Vygotsky, 1978, 1986), need access to their physical concrete worlds. The movements of his hand, and some language ("I made it high"), gave Leonard a developmentally appropriate start in his symbolic exploration. Further, as the "expert other" (Bruner, 1986; Vygotsky, 1978, 1986), I caught on to Leonard's exploration of symbols and dimensionality just in time to write down his gesture squiggles and help scaffold his work.

LITERACY AS ACTION

Literacy as action refers to children's interest in both the internal movement and action of books and stories, and also how children use their interest in action to make sense of literacy activities. I often used small figures and other manipulative props when reading books with the children. When I read *Cat on the Mat* (Wildsmith, 1982), I had the children hold the animal characters and place them on a small felt mat as the simple story progressed. From time to time, I embellished the story to make the language more sophisticated and make more involved use of the figures and props for the children. I changed the story so that the main character of the cat was "lonely and sad and had no friends"—this piqued the children's interest and their desire to help the cat have friends. "One day," I said, "along came some animals and they all wanted to sit on the cat's mat." I then continued as the cat allowed each animal onto her mat until it "got so noisy that she scared them away," and then realized that "she enjoyed the calm and quiet of her mat all by herself." I ended the story with the cat declaring, "Finally, now I have some peace and quiet." (One time, I asked the children what this meant. John said, "That's what my momma says when my baby brother is asleep.") After our small group readings, the children loved using the plastic animals to tell the story. On one occasion, LaTeesha and Shatani used the animals and the mat to retell the story. LaTeesha held the book open for both of them and turned to the appropriate page, while Shatani held the animals to be placed on the small mat. Both girls worked on the floor while I read with another child nearby. What I have put in quotation marks below signifies what the animals are saying to each other.

LaTeesha: You have to make it [plastic animal] say, "Can I get on your mat?"
Shatani: The elephant said, "Can I get on the mat, please?"
LaTeesha: Shatani, let's have a party and say, "Can I sit on your mat?" (restarting the animal's dialogue with this new story line) "Can I sit on your mat?"
Shatani: "Yes, please."

In this scene, LaTeesha and Shatani's manipulation of the action of the story through the animal figures helps build their interest in the book and in their joint collaboration in recreating the story. At the beginning of their collaboration, LaTeesha's comment that "you have to make it [plastic animal] say, 'Can I get on your mat?'" reminds Shatani to use the linguistic routine that I modeled for the children. After starting from my model, LaTeesha quickly redirects the language and the action by suggesting, "Shatani, let's have a party and say, 'Can I sit on your mat?'" In effect, LaTeesha plays the more expert other (Vygotsky, 1978, 1986) to scaffold the children's literacy engagement with the story. LaTeesha helps direct the activity and dialogue in a new creative way based on her talents for using language in concert and collaboration with her peers. LaTeesha's efforts could be seen as just social manipulation of the situation; but Shatani didn't appear to think so, taking LaTeesha's use of the subjunctive "let's" as a true invitation, and the two children happily went on with the new story line about having a party.

The children also are experimenting with the extent to which it is fun and satisfying to play at the boundaries of interactional and linguistic routines in literacy learning. I set the initial routine in motion by modeling for the children the basic dialogue and action of the plastic animal figures in the story. The dual experiences of my initial modeling and the children's independent collaboration allowed the children developmental space to recreate the story's action and a sense of responsiveness through animal roles and voices ("You have to make it [plastic animal] say, 'Can I get on your mat?'") and social collaboration ("Let's have a party"). Further, both experiences helped deepen the element of addressivity, or "the quality of turning toward someone" (Bakhtin, 1986, p. 99) between the children and the basic routine, the larger story, the plastic animals, their peers, and the inner language of story and the outer language of literacy experience (Hicks, 1998). In this last way, LaTeesha and Shatani's particular attention to the book can be seen as a "social interactional process" in "which learners come to appropriate textual forms in school through social dialogue with others" (Hicks, 1998, p. 31).

The children also appropriated their personal experiences in the world outside of school to heighten their social interest in literacy as action. One morning, Curtis, David, and Tawana worked in their journals at the same table. As he drew, David looked at an *Eyewitness* (Macquitty, 1992) shark book in front of him.

TAWANA: He'll [the shark on the page] gobble you up.
CURTIS: Sharks is not real in books.
DAVID: (joining in) They're real at Marine World [local animal theme park]. Marine World is gonna be bad [on upcoming school field trip].
CURTIS: The last time I went to Marine World with my granny, I saw an elephant.

According to the developing sound and sense of these four-year-olds, the children dispute any hard-and-fast division between fact and fiction, book sharks and real sharks. For Tawana, sharks are real on the illustrated page and not only can move but can leap off the page and bite you. For Curtis, sharks are not real in books because they can't possibly move and bite. For David, sharks are real and can move in the real world of experience at Marine World. Although sharing a common literacy space at the table, the children have their own individual interpretations of the closeness (and realness) of the movement of book characters and the movement of real-life experience. Sharks, then, can be "real" in books *and* on paper *and* in children's conversations *and* at Marine Worlds past and present and future.

Given the children's varied interpretations of the degree to which real life and book life correspond, it makes good pedagogical sense for Tawana and her classmates to be exposed to a variety of literacy borders (Gutierrez & Larson, 1994) and scripts (Hatch, 1992). The developmental and responsive aspects of the children's literacy engagement are revealed, then, in the varied and extended opportunities for children to shape their own borders and make their own literacy scripts in reaction to and alongside those of their teachers. The children enjoy and profit from early experience in discovering the makeup of literary texts (Curtis: "Sharks is not real in books") and how these texts stack up against what they know from the outside world (David: "They're real at Marine World"). And the big test for children of this age comes in the literary focus of action and what propels the action and movement of a book or a story. Tawana and her friends immerse themselves in multiple quandaries—sharks move at Marine World so they're real; sharks don't move in books so they're not real; and (added by Curtis) sharks are real because elephants are real, too. The literary action of books then becomes the social action of the children's social engagement—debating the realness of book life versus the realness of experiential life, the children affirm and strengthen the potential of the group for literary inquiry and social cohesiveness.

In focusing on literacy as action, I also wanted to promote the children's sensitivity toward the narrative action of stories and books. I wanted the children, for instance, to look for the reappearing cat in *Ten, Nine, Eight* (Bang, 1983), to search for each newly appearing animal hiding in *The Mitten* (Brett, 1989), to ponder why the child is crying on the cover of *The Old Man & His Door* (Soto, 1996), to share secrets about making friends as depicted in *Yo! Yes!* (Raschka, 1993). In order to promote the children's interests in and talents for narrative action, I helped the children make new kinds of connections between narrative action and children's active worlds of experience.

The children loved to play with the boundaries of narrative and nonfiction. One day, as I sat with Paris to do her dictation at the computer, I had in mind for her to dictate a fictional story, which I would type for her. Paris, though, reached for a nearby book about barn owls that I had read with the children. She wanted to do her dictation based on the barn owl book. By selecting the owl book as the basis for her story, Paris appropriated the foundation for the content and the action of her text-to-be. Looking at the book, turning the pages about barn owl life, Paris proceeded to put her own narrative of action on the science book.

The barn owl flew and flew. He then went down down down.
He made a place. He lived in a barn on a farm. He went
hunting at nighttime. Then there were some baby barn owls.
They cracked out of the eggs. They grew bigger and bigger. They
started to fly. The dad gave them some food. The babies had long
wings and flew up in the sky. The End

Paris used the built-in structure and foundation of the barn owl book for her storying; the unfolding story of the pictures provided a scaffold (Bruner, 1986) for Paris, although rather than "an adult or more capable peer" (Vygotsky, 1978), she led herself on without my prompting or cueing. In this way, Paris provided a *self-scaffold* for herself within my general dictation routine, and the book (and the real-world life of barn owls) became her dialogical peer and partner. Through her unfolding narrative script about the owls, Paris essentially talked the barn owls into being and talked her way into and out of the book. In so doing, Paris transported us from the urban world of Hawthorne Preschool to the rural world of barn owls depicted in the book.

Sitting behind us, Joseph witnessed Paris's creation and followed her lead by selecting one of his favorite shark books for his dictation.

> The shark pulled him [man in photograph in the book] out of the water. The boy touched the teeth. The shark was swimming. The shark is turning in the water. He jumped out of the water. There is a hammerhead shark. There are different kinds of sharks. Sharks look for food. The End

Like Paris, Joseph added action and drama and movement to the still-life photographs of the sharks. Talking his way into the world of sharks, Joseph upended the genre of the book by going back and forth between the language of stories ("The shark pulled him out of the water") and the language of science and information books ("There are different kinds of sharks"). As Paris and Joseph play with the action potential of the texts, they help themselves toward a greater sense of addressivity and a greater "multivoicedness of meaning" (Wertsch, 1991) in their literacy engagement. Although not reading in a conventional sense, Paris and Joseph rely on their oral language powers and interest in the action of texts to bring more voices to the literacy activity and gain a more meaningful connection to the books.

LITERACY AS POWER

Literacy as power refers to the possibilities for school literacy to support and strengthen children's personal and cultural identities. One day, Veronica started to draw in her journal when she announced to her table mates, "Y'all better like mine. Mine's gonna be hecka good." On another occasion, Isis drew a simple human figure in her journal. For her dictation, Isis said, "She's a teenager. She's not grown. She can go to school by herself. She's going to the store. It's not dark yet. She never ever go to a store that's closed." Before she even starts her work, Veronica gets the attention of her peers with her announcement, "Y'all better like mine." After finishing her drawing, Isis's dictation creates a mini-world about an older teenager who "can go to school by herself" even though "she's not grown." For Veronica and Isis, playing with and discovering the power of literacy helps them gain social membership and strengthen their identities for themselves and with others.

What kind of literacy power, though, do children want? By linking language, literacy, and identity the children show their desire for literacy to form critical communal and social ties (Delgado-Gaitan, 1996; Delpit, 1995; Taylor, 1997; Valdés, 1996). In playing with the potential of literacy to influence power relations with others, the children use literacy to influence their membership within the "child collective" (Bruner, 1986) and their evolving "peer culture" (Corsaro, 1985). And since schools are becoming increasingly complicated social and cultural places, the children show how literacy can help them cross boundaries and strengthen their social and cultural ties.

The children and I read and discussed various versions of the Little Red Hen such as *The Little Red Hen: An Old Story* (Zemach, 1983) and *Red Hen and Sly Fox* (French, 1994). The children loved the predictability and the structured text of the classic story, and they enjoyed changing the dialogue and lines as I sometimes substituted, "Because we have better things to do," after the hen's, "Who would like to help me?" instead of the book's, "Not I, said the goose. Not I, said the cat. Not I, said the pig."

After we read the story, I asked the children if it was fair of the hen not to share her food with her friends.

TYESHA: No, they're your friends. You should give them some.

EMERALD: She should give them some.

EMILE: No, they're not going to be friends.

ROBERT: No, because the friends didn't make the thing or do nothing.

MARVIN: No, because she ain't give them no food. They didn't help her.

EMERALD: (contributing again) No, it's not fair. They didn't help her plant the grain or do the flour either.

MR. MEIER: What if they [animals] said, "We'll help you next time, but can we have some bread now?"

EMERALD: Yes, that'd be OK.

Asking the children whether the hen's decision to withhold bread was warranted or not makes good developmental sense and promotes responsiveness to the story. The children were able and eager to discuss the morality of the story's plot because friendship and sharing are important topics and often are at the center of peer power struggles. The children also enjoyed contributing their opinions because of the potential of these issues to strengthen the "child collective" (Bruner, 1986) and "peer culture" (Corsaro, 1985).

After we read and discussed the book, I asked Emile, Tyesha, and Gerardo to use a batch of play dough to make their own bread as a concrete extension of the story. As I read with the other children, I observed the children playing with the play dough. I had thought they would enjoy the activity and anticipated that they would roll and knead the play dough into different shapes of bread. And this is exactly what the children did do. A few minutes later, though, I saw Emile, Tyesha, and Gerardo leaning over the play dough on the table. The children were making an interesting discovery. They were leaning over the table and pressing their jacket zippers and sweater buttons on the pieces of play dough bread, and pulling away and marveling at their imprints left on the dough. They were delighted with themselves. What I had set out as a concrete connection to the Red Hen story, the children transformed into an even more concrete one, which had greater power to engage the children socially than the bread making.

The children publicly exerted their power to create and reinterpret the form, function, and content of our literacy work in still other situations. On another occasion, I sat with Tremel, Isis, Rosa, and Aaron to do dictation on the computer. After I suggested several possible topics for Tremel, he finally decided to tell about what he wanted "to be when he grew up." He dictated, "I want to be Michael Jordan. I want to dunk the ball." Hearing Tremel's intentions, Isis followed and also took up the when-I-grow-up theme. She declared, "I want to be a mommy. I want to be a kindergarten teacher and teach kids how to draw a businessperson."

Tremel's and Isis's dictations reveal the power of literary text making in school settings for trying on adult roles—"to dunk a basketball" and "to be a mommy" and "a kindergarten teacher"—and to be tickled with the power possibilities of literacy to influence and control their future selves. Tremel and Isis use literacy to play with time and human growth, speeding up their four-year-old lives to reach adulthood and "dunk a basketball" and "teach kids how to draw a businessperson." For Tremel and Isis, and the majority of the other children who were enamored with their older siblings and wanted "to get bigger," literacy can help transform traditional boundaries of development and identity.

This playing with time and development also is rooted in the children's cultural and communal affiliations with friends, family, and other respected people. For Tremel, sitting down with me at the computer offers the opportunity to exhibit the cultural power of wanting to grow up to "be like

Mike [Jordan]" (Ladson-Billings, 1998, p. 62)—and the potential power of the linking of texts, school, and social relationships with "the power of African American male culture" (p. 62). In wanting to be like Mike, Tremel jumps time zones of child development and identity, connecting himself with a contemporary icon who symbolizes power, grace, success, and supreme confidence. Sitting at the computer, waiting for Tremel to dictate, I had not the slightest notion that Tremel would make the leap from four-year-old to adult and from Tremel-the-child to Tremel-as-Michael Jordan. By taking control of the initial movement of his short dictated text, by exercising a sense of power over his text-to-be, Tremel mirrors the power and control of Michael Jordan—he and Michael both soar and swoop at some future date and in some future identity. In effect, Tremel draws a line between himself as child and his vision of himself as adult through a simple text. And suddenly, two sentences later, Tremel is larger than life, transformed into the icon of envy and admiration of both children and adults alike: Michael Jordan.

The children are also eager to play with the literacy power to be found in their early drawings and written language explorations. Working in his journal, Kahlil drew several wavy lines across his page in different marker colors. Pointing to each of the three different lines, he said, "This is my name in cursive." "This is me." "This is Mr. Meier." By identifying his name, himself, and me, Kahlil took the initiative in using the same wavy lines to stand for three quite dissimilar objects and people. The opportunity to explore the page with others, and the possibility to discuss his work-in-progress with me, strengthened Kahlil's efforts and interest in melding the social and the representational. Playing with repeated lines and the generative aspect of children's early writing (Clay, 1975), Kahlil plays with the power of the same simple wavy lines to symbolize and represent different parts of his immediate intellectual and social world. So rather than the common teacherly push for children to categorize and group what is similar, Kahlil looks for what is dissimilar as a way of linking and connecting the known of human experience with the representational potential of symbols (Donaldson, 1978). He discovers, too, the power of literacy to serve as once- and twice-removed (Vygotsky, 1978, 1986) symbols of his experience and his moment-by-moment interpretation of his world as it changes.

On another occasion, Toneece drew a picture in her journal and then asked me how to write my name.

TONEECE: How you spell your name?
MR. MEIER: M-R-M [my child abbreviation for Mr. Meier]
TONEECE: Is that all?
MR. MEIER: Yes. (Toneece writes the letters and starts to draw me)

TONEECE: First I'm going to make your shoes. OK, so there are your
    shoes. Now you're skating. (drawing the rest of me) I'm going to
    color the inside of your stomach.
SHABRE: (sitting beside Toneece, and incredulous) How you gonna do
    that?

For Toneece, the literal act of writing and drawing me (and Shabre)
on her written and drawn page pulled us into a shared social situation.
She did so through the use of questions ("How you spell your name?")
and literacy action ("First I'm going to make your shoes"). In the process,
Toneece appropriated an important measure of control and power over
the social and literary direction of the activity. Announcing, "I'm going
to color the inside of your stomach," Toneece even prompted Shabre to
ask, "How you gonna do that?" Like with a magic show, Shabre became
interested because Toneece's language and literacy played along the boundaries of the real world and the depicted world. In this sense, to the mind of
a four-year-old, it's one thing to talk about the inside of Mr. Meier's stomach and quite another to really draw his stomach! Toneece and Shabre,
although in different ways, sense the literacy power of playing along this
boundary.

On another occasion, Ashley drew in her journal as she engaged me
and her classmates in conversation.

ASHLEY: You want me to tell you what I'm making?
MR. MEIER: Yes.
ASHLEY: I'm making a flower. (turning to Ti'ana, seated beside her) You
    know how to make a flower? (Ti'ana nods) You want to spell
    some words? (Ti'ana nods again, and Ashley writes "cat," "dog,"
    "book")
MR. MEIER: Did you ask your mom to write the words, or did your
    mom say that she wanted you to learn them?
ASHLEY: I asked my mom to teach me how to spell them.
MR. MEIER: How come?
ASHLEY: I want to be smart.

Ashley senses the social and intellectual power of literacy for creating a
bond with adults ("You want me to tell you what I'm making?") and for
sharing and teaching with peers ("You know how to make a flower?"). Like
Veronica's opening line, "Y'all better like mine," Ashley also has the idea
that literacy-in-the-making can garner the attention of others. It can serve
as a powerful and effective way to gain social contact with other children
and with adults in developmentally appropriate and responsive ways.
Ashley knows, too, that conventional writing is "a code of power" (Delpit,

1995), which is central for school success and literacy achievement. In literacy activities that promote opportunities for children to gain some measure of skill in literacy, children like Ashley learn that school-based literacy itself has the power to make connections with home. The opportunity to spell and write words, and to do so with others in a social and public way in the classroom, goes a long way toward honoring the wishes and expectations of home.

TOWARD A LONG VIEW OF LITERACY EDUCATION

A long view of literacy education turns the recurring emphasis on the single best practices and methods toward a vision of literacy teaching as an art and a creative endeavor by both adults and children. Language arts teaching is essentially a human relationship (Ashton-Warner, 1963) that touches intimate issues of cultural identity (Delgado-Gaitan, 1996; Delpit, 1995; Igoa, 1995; Ladson-Billings, 1994; Valdés, 1996) and the magic of stories and narrative (Britsch, 1994; Bruner, 1994; Coles, 1989; Paley, 1981; Rosen, 1977). It is not easily boxed and transported across time and space and cultural contexts. Rather, it needs to be grounded within the local and personal relationships among children, between children and adults, and between children and the words and images of literacy.

When we read *Snowballs* (Ehlert, 1995) and I asked the children about a pile of birdseed on the ground (with no bird feeder pictured), Lavon said, "My grandma got one of those things [bird feeder] and she put it outside." Lavon's comment links the book with his concrete physical experience of the bird feeder in his grandmother's yard. When David, Curtis, and Tawana discuss sharks and Marine World (Curtis: "Sharks is not real in books," and David: "They're real at Marine World"), the children reveal the role of action in their playing along their newly discovered boundaries and scripts of literacy in school. Writing my name and drawing me ("I'm going to color the inside of your stomach"), Toneece indicates the power of literacy to influence social relationships and engage peers and adults in the fictional and creative worlds of childhood.

I select these three aspects of children's literacy attachment as a collective way to remind us of the roots of children's school-based literary experiences. As a teacher, I watch for symbols and symbol-making possibilities that can promote children's literacy learning. The children, although willing to go along with me, are often closer to something more elemental, something more akin to the mix of literacy as physical, action, and power. For instance, when I used small objects and figures while reading books, I saw the children's affinity for grasping, playing with, and moving these objects. When we used felt pieces of food for *The Very Hungry Caterpillar*

(Carle, 1969), I placed the pieces in a row on the floor as I read about each item of food in the book. The children, though, spontaneously placed each piece of food right onto its drawn representation in the book. When I later read the book with David and Lavon, David decided to hold the large felt caterpillar with a large mouth opening while Lavon held the pile of food pieces. I thought that David and Lavon would place the objects in the caterpillar's mouth. What happened was slightly different; as I mentioned each kind of food from the book, Lavon handed the appropriate piece of food to David, who put it up to the caterpillar's mouth, paused as if to let the caterpillar eat, and then put the piece of food down. In this way, Lavon and David acted out their own version of developmentally appropriate and responsive practice; they used pretend play to make concrete connections with the story (putting the food to the caterpillar's mouth), and used their own child-created ways for collaborating socially (breaking down the language and the narrative by sharing the objects and action).

Lavon and David and their classmates need to stay close to the roots of literacy as framed and guided by teachers in creative, richly constructed literacy activities. The roots of literacy reveal children's affinity for literacy as physical, action, and power. This kind of attention, then, to the early literate lives of children reveals a wonderfully messy place for seeing literacy as peculiarly human, at times frustratingly idiosyncratic, at times moving and changing too fast for step-by-step teacherly prodding and direction.

The children also remind us that we gather around books and texts and drawings in schools to gain greater intimacy, a greater sense of place and inclusiveness for ourselves and each other. The children show that our varied imprints of literacy use and orientation—whether influenced by gender, ethnicity, culture, language, experience, or other factors—can jump (like Michael Jordan) boundaries and make personal connections for children.

Although I have separated literacy as physical, action, and power—for they are but abstractions in our adult minds—the hearts and thoughts of the children move more in concert, more connected and integrated. As in Joseph's excited claim, "I'm him. I'm him. I'm him," in taking the role of all three of the big-book dinosaurs at once, literacy in the preschool knows few boundaries of form, style, content, and tradition. Literacy moves as children move, as their drawing and talking about *The Lion King* is all the rage one moment and out the next, replaced by *Toy Story* or *The Prince of Egypt*. As children move, teachers and other adults scramble to stay within distance, reshaping old literate scenes and shaping new ones for children. Children, then, are never ready for literacy; they're both never ready and always ready. It's the best kind of paradox for children.

Chapter 4

Scribble Scrabble–Tensions of Form and Function

> This is when the monkeys in the scribble scrabble got dizzy. They said, "Oh dear, what is that?" It has orange people and filled with scribble scrabble. They got dizzy and dizzy and dizzy.
> —Tammy's dictation for her journal drawing

Who ever heard of monkeys getting dizzy in scribble scrabble, children's apparently random and nonrepresentational drawings and writing? Who ever heard of scribble scrabble as a fictional character? By bringing scribble scrabble into her story as a central protagonist, Tammy shows how children want to cross adult constructions of acceptable and developmental literacy development. In observing and talking with the children about scribble scrabble, I found that the children's actions and perspectives show a rich variety of orientations toward possible new forms and functions for school literacy.

As much as we may wish to view children as developing readers and writers, children themselves see the value of literacy in intimate relation to their evolving identities and personal relationships with family, friends, and teachers. In teaching the children, I organized and framed my literacy activities to play upon the children's interest in forging a dynamic relationship between language and interaction (Bruner, 1986; Vygotsky, 1978, 1986) through strengthening their personal and cultural identities (Delgado-Gaitan, 1996; Delpit, 1995; Ladson-Billings, 1994). Children want to be, in their own eyes and in the eyes of others, accepted as competent and successful members of their intellectual and social worlds. They want to be accepted for who they already are and, at the same time, also accepted for who they are expected to become in classrooms. I used literacy activities to strengthen children's emerging sense of communicative competence (Hymes, 1972), or their ability and knowledge for successfully using language in socially and culturally expected ways with others. As I designed literacy activities to expand children's communicative competence, I learned to see how certain tensions of literary form and function reveal the children's strong desire for social and intellectual inclusion.

CHILDREN'S PERSPECTIVES ON SCHOOL LITERACY

The children held definite ideas and perspectives on what language arts learning meant to them and on what they could and couldn't do with literacy in school.

MR. MEIER: What are the ABCs?
TASHA: Numbers.
TINELLE: When you get bigger, you can learn the ABCs.
RYSHEA: It's alphabets.
JONELLE: They look like alphabets.
DALISA: Teachers will tell your ABCs and big people [too].
TYRONE: Alphabets. ABCs. (he sings the alphabet song)

The children wanted to learn literacy in school and recognized the importance of literacy skills associated with the alphabet. The children also sensed that literacy competency was tied to their general developmental growth (the traditional "ages and stages" of child development) and to expectations from families, teachers, and other children (social and communal influences on language use). For instance, many of the four-year-old children were convinced that it was perfectly appropriate for three-year-olds and even younger children to scribble scrabble, but inappropriate for them as older children; they admitted doing scribble scrabble when they "were little," but now they were older and knew better. In this distancing of past and present markers of literacy development, the children were keen to state for the record where they had been, where they were, and where they needed to go in their literacy education.

From Home to School (and Back Again)

I overheard Jeremiah tell Ashayah, "I did scribble scrabble." To which Ashayah replied, "You're going to have a dream about it at home." In these and other comments and actions as the children drew and conversed, I saw scribble scrabble as a window onto social and cultural perspectives on literacy use in home and school. As I tried to understand the children's perspectives on scribble scrabble, I learned that the children have their own particular views on appropriate and responsive literacy education.

MR. MEIER: Can you scribble scrabble in school?
BRITTNEY: Yes. If the teacher won't see you, you can scribble scrabble.
ALEXA: My mommy doesn't want me to scribble scrabble in school.
QUNEESE: I don't like to scribble scrabble. I don't know how to scribble

scrabble. Little little kids can scribble. The kids [three-year-olds across the hallway] can do better [than scribble scrabble].

LANI: You're supposed to draw a picture and write your name [rather than scribble scrabble].

TIFFANY: 'Cuz you need to write your name.

LANI: Room 1 [three-year-olds] can scribble scrabble. They don't know how to write.

TIFFANY: We're big kids.

JONELLE: I'm make mines [drawings] pretty. You can do anything with your paper like bad or good.

SARAH: Some of our friends scribble scrabble. The teachers tell us not to scribble scrabble. We're not supposed to.

In talking with the children's teachers, which I discuss later, I found that the teachers were not uniformly against scribble scrabble or entirely in favor of encouraging the children to mark, draw, and write just as they wished. In speaking with the parents, which I also discuss later, I discovered that they wanted the children to have play and developmental experiences and also to learn certain literacy and numeracy skills. For some teachers, scribble scrabble became an issue as part of a larger general focus on socialization into language and literacy and general school behavior. In the schools, then, learning how to do literacy is as important as learning what to do with literacy.

Scribble scrabble also formed a strong part of the children's social cohesion, serving as a source of both strong disagreement and agreement as the children participated in language and literacy activities. One day, as I worked with a small group of children, Makisha and Keith drew in their journals together at a table in the library.

MAKISHA: I do pretty stuff.

KEITH: (to Makisha) Is this scribble scrabble?

MAKISHA: (inspecting Keith's drawing and writing for several seconds) It look like it, but it ain't.

I asked again about scribble scrabble.

KEITH: Scribble scrabble is when you don't color right. Room 1 can do scribble scrabble.

MAKISHA: You turn pages and you ask the teacher if you can have another paper. That's how you do scribble scrabble. Ask Bob [preschool teacher for the three-year-olds at Hawthorne] if you can have another piece of paper and another paper. That's how you do scribble scrabble. Ask the teacher if you can have another piece of paper. You ask nicely. You do one paper—one by one. You're supposed to listen to the teacher. I do pretty stuff.

For Makisha, scribble scrabble is what you do when you rush ("You turn pages"), while the more appropriate behavior is to take your time and work carefully ("You do one paper—one by one"). Since Makisha believes that it is important to "ask the teacher nicely" for more paper, and hints at the value of slow and careful work, she points to scribble scrabble as one part literacy learning and one part appropriate school behavior. What is acceptable and appropriate to draw and write on paper, then, is intimately tied to appropriate school behavior. School socialization and school literacy influence each other; the road to social acceptance within the school culture is closely connected with the road to literacy learning and development.

Scribble scrabble also indicates the children's interest in growing older and "getting bigger," and going beyond their chronological age. This interest in getting bigger surfaced in our conversations about scribble scrabble.

EVA: You're supposed to draw a nice picture. An ugly picture if you
    scribble scrabble.
GENEVA: It's [scribble scrabble] out of the lines.
DANIEL: Like this. (holds up his picture)
AKARRAH: Like this. (draws quickly across the page)
GENEVA: Little kids can scribble scrabble, but Eva is not a little kid.
EVA: I'll never be a little kid again.

As I worked with the four- and five-year-old children, many of the three-year-olds in the classrooms also wanted to work with me. I sometimes told these children that I'd work with them "next year, when you're bigger." Some of these children seized the idea, on the very next day when I walked into their classrooms, of informing me, "Mr. Meier, I'm bigger now." This interest in getting bigger was part of the children's interest in growing up, in going beyond their chronological years and their supposed developmental capabilities with language and literacy. Many of the children also had older brothers and sisters and relatives and neighbors, and often talked about doing things with these older family members and helping to take care of even younger siblings and neighbors' children.

TEXT STRATEGIES FOR LITERACY COMPETENCY AND SOCIAL INCLUSION

From home and school, the preschoolers learn that there are certain goals and behaviors indicating success and progress with school literacy.

They learn, too, that growing up and being accepted into the child collective (Bruner, 1986) and peer culture (Corsaro, 1985) are powerfully influenced by children's participation in the accepted and expected literacy scripts and school routines for literacy use. In learning to recognize and manipulate these scripts for acceptance by adults and inclusion by peers, the children experience a performative process of social acceptance and literary expression. Children's performative styles (Dyson, 1993), or the expression of the nuances of language and discourse, help children gain acceptance and inclusion as up-and-coming, ready-to-go literacy interpreters and users. As I worked with the children, I found that book reading and book sharing provided an important social and academic forum for practicing and demonstrating the performance of language and literacy in school. In these highly social and interactive experiences with books, which most often happened during the children's independent reading time, the children employed starting off (SO) and in-text (IT) strategies to promote social inclusion and literacy competence.

Starting Off Strategies

In the fourth part of our small group literacy work, when the children chose books to read on their own or with me or other children, I discovered that the children used a rich and effective array of strategies for starting off their book reading and sharing. It is important to remember that all of the approximately 300 children whom I taught (except for only one child) could not actually decode or read the books. How, then, did the children find the confidence and the skill to "read" and talk about books in public without knowing how to read in a conventional sense? How did they get over this potential source of frustration, and how did they get beyond their interest in "getting bigger" and learning how to read like "big kids"? The children's inventions of several starting off strategies helped them get right into a book and quickly get over any initial complaints to me such as, "But I can't read, Mr. Meier" or "I don't know how to read."

SO #1: Acknowledge that a peer or would-be friend has the same book. For example, Juan, a Spanish speaker gaining fluency in English, said to LaTeesha, "You have the same book as me." Juan was reading a small version of *Dinosaurs, Dinosaurs* (Barton, 1989), while LaTeesha held the big-book version of the same title. Juan's comment was a perfect invitation and "way in" to sharing the books together; Juan and LaTeesha then sat down side by side on the rug to compare books and talk as they read. The children thus shared the same book while each holding and reading a copy.

How can teachers and parents support and nurture this strategy of sharing books with other children? First, it was helpful to provide opportunities for children to browse through the books and select their own books for reading and discussion. Second, the library at Hawthorne had two copies each of several book titles, and when I brought a bookbag full of books to the other preschools, I often brought two copies of the same book. It was helpful, though, to have only two copies of the same book; otherwise, it was a less satisfying and surprising discovery for the children when they found the two matching book titles. Third, it was also beneficial to have a small-book and a big-book version of the same book title, as the children loved discovering that the same book could come in such different sizes and still be the same story.

SO #2: Act like a teacher and turn the book teacher-style so that an audience can see the illustrations and listen to the story. This strategy has a few variations: (1) there is no need for an actual audience of other children; (2) a few children can simultaneously read *different* books from their chairs to an imaginary audience; (3) you can just start reading and, if you line up a few extra chairs, someone might soon join you; and (4) you can even do this on the computer by turning the book toward the computer screen as the computer "reads" a CD-ROM version of the book. For example, Lani turned a chair around in the Hawthorne library and proceeded to read a made-up-on-the-spot version of *Clean Up Your Room, Harvey Moon!* (Cummings, 1991). As she read, Lani paused to show the illustrations to her imaginary audience.

To support this strategy, I found it helpful to allow children to choose their own books and to make available the books that I had just read. This enabled the children to have a fresh story to read, and a familiar script that they either had memorized or could improvise a new version of based on my reading. Further, if the book proved quite popular with the other children, the child who wanted to read the book also might get an actual audience (other than an imagined one) for the rereading. Last, it was helpful to set up only a few chairs (to simulate a teacher's chair) for the children to use for reading teacher-style and to have room on the rug for a small audience. The children never needed my assistance in carrying out this child-created strategy, and rarely did they argue over who got to read and who got to be in the audience; they enjoyed enacting both roles.

SO #3: Use kid lingo or the language of the peer culture as a one- or two-line book review. This strategy, which involved children recommending books to each other, promoted child-to-child interest in books as an initial hook into selecting and reading a book either alone or with peers. For example, Aman selected a book about the circus and said to Jonathan, "Let's look at this book. This book is *tight*." On another occasion, Gerardo selected a science book about dinosaurs and said to Kahlil, "Hey, read Jurassic Park. I got Jurassic Park. It was *too* hot." In the first instance, Aman combined an overt invitation to read ("Let's look at this book") along with a popular description of something fun and cool ("This book is *tight*"). Jonathan took him up on his offer and they sat down to read together. In the second example, Gerardo combined an overt suggestion for reading a book ("Hey, read Jurassic Park") along with calling the dinosaur book a popular movie for children (*Jurassic Park*) and more kid lingo ("It was *too* hot"). Not able to pass up such a peer review, Kahlil took the dinosaur book.

Both instances of this strategy can be supported by allowing children to talk and interact during the very first moments when they select books for reading. A "no talking while you get books" rule defeats this purpose. It was also helpful to bring in books that addressed favorite topics for children, such as any kind of dinosaur or shark book. I also found it helpful to refer children to other children whom I knew liked the book—"Go ask Julio about that book. He liked it," or "Ask Alice. She really liked that book and maybe she'll even read it with you." These kinds of comments on my part helped the children help each other start off their independent book sharing.

SO #4: Ask an adult or another child to find the books known by the children's own descriptions for the real titles. These child-created names included the "wolf book" (*Lon Po Po*, Young, 1989), "the rabbit book" (*Zomo the Rabbit*, McDermott, 1992), "the spider book" (*Anansi the Spider*, McDermott, 1972), "the caterpillar book" (*The Very Hungry Caterpillar*, Carle, 1969), "the coconut book" (*Chicka Chicka Boom Boom*, Martin & Archambault, 1989), the "sad cat" book (*Cat on the Mat*, Wildsmith, 1982), the "alligator book" (my set of 26 12" x 12" alphabet pictures on two metal rings starting with an alligator for "A"), or "the one that has a blue dog, and a red bird, and a purple cat" (*Brown Bear, Brown Bear*, Martin & Carle, 1967).

This strategy indicated children's interest in selecting and reading books that were favorites within the peer group. The children's use of their own child-created titles served to reinforce this interest. I supported this strategy by remembering which books the children's titles referred to and keeping track of where the books were so that I could easily help the children find the books. In addition, it was helpful to cultivate crowd favorites (the "sad cat book" or "the rabbit book") through my reading and re-reading of certain books; this gave the children the sense over time that the books could be favorites with the children and with the teacher.

In-Text Strategies

The starting off strategies got the children off to a good beginning, helping them make the transition from our drawing and writing activities to independent reading. At this point, the children employed a number of their own in-text strategies, which further propelled their reading.

IT #1: Repeat small, manageable chunks of text language. For example, Zariah brought me *There's a Sea in My Bedroom* (Wild, 1987) and wanted me to read it. As I started, she spontaneously joined in. Zariah, who spoke Hindi and had a beginning command of English, started to repeat every sentence that I read. After a few pages, I started to pause after I read a sentence in order to let her repeat the sentence and practice the English sentence construction and sound. On another occasion, Juan, a Spanish speaker learning English, used the same strategy as he repeated each phrase I read from *Go Away, Big Green Monster!* (Emberley, 1993). With glee, Juan loved to repeat the line, "Go away, big green monster!" which appears on only two pages, as he turned *every single page* of the book.

I supported this strategy by making sure we had suitable books with small chunks of text, somewhat simple sentence construction and vocabulary, at least one catchy line ("Go away, big green monster!"), and large illustrations. These texts helped children repeat each sentence without feeling overloaded with complex syntax and vocabulary, and the illustrations gave the children more information and background for understanding the message of the text. Supporting this strategy was particularly useful for children learning English, as it gave added opportunities to scaffold text and practice fluency.

IT #2: Solicit adult or child assistance in order to keep the flow of the story going. This strategy helped the children maintain the story line that they had either memorized or were improvising so they could continue reading the book. For instance, Brittney sat down with the big-book version of the story *Three Billy Goats Gruff* (Smith & Parkes, 1986), turned to the first page, and in a big deep voice said, "Who is that walking on . . . [pause] who is that walking onto my ba-ridge [drawn out first syllable for dramatic effect]?" Then she added, "Hey I can't . . . Mr. Meier, can you read this part? Mr. Meier, can you read this part?" Since I was busy, another child, Mia, helped out and repeated Brittney's last line back to her, "'Who's that walking over my bridge.' That's what you said." This helped Brittney get back on track in her reading.

This in-text strategy can be fostered by initially helping children learn the repeated lines of text and conversation in books and stories ("Who is that walking on my bridge" for *Three Billy Goats Gruff*; "Who's going to help me _____" for *The Little Red Hen*). Once children learn these chunks of language with other children in a small group setting, saying the lines in chorus with others, the children then have the opportunity during independent reading to try out this strategy of soliciting help from others. Occasionally, children did not overtly ask for assistance, but simply paused and looked at me or a peer for assistance.

IT #3: Use traditional formulaic story openers ("once upon a time") and endings ("and they lived happily ever after" and "they went to sleep") during any part of a book and even when the book isn't a fairy tale or doesn't even have a happy ending. For instance, Jamaal read a book on trucks and said, "Once upon a time," before he turned each page to describe a new truck. Jamaal delighted in the repeated phrase "once upon a time," which apparently gave him both a rhythm and a chance to create a mini-story on each page. On another occasion, while reading *Fish Eyes* (Ehlert, 1992), which I had read as a counting book, Julio (a bilingual Spanish/English speaker) started each page by saying, "Once upon a time . . ." and then counted the total number of fish on the page. Like Jamaal, Julio used this formulaic story opener to create a mini-story on each page of the book and to combine the language of fairy tales with the genre of counting books.

I supported this strategy by reading books that included these kinds of formulaic beginnings and endings. Once I saw how the children used these phrases at any time during a book reading, I started to do the same. This helped reinforce a strategy invented by the children, and they loved hearing me use their idea. I also strengthened possibilities for this strategy by changing the formulaic and predictable text in stories—in *The Little Red Hen* (Zemach, 1983), I inserted a new line for the hen's friends ("Not me. I got *better* things to do") rather than the given "Not I" when the hen asked, "Who's going to help me?" The children learned the given book version ("Not I") and also my version ("Not me. I got *better* things to do"). This increased children's experiences with playing with formulaic phrases and increased the repertoire of phrases for their own reading.

IT #4: Explain, in one grand theory or comment, the crux of a book's plot or a character's predicament. This strategy helped the children sum up, explain, or question crucial parts of a book or story. Michael, reading *The Very Hungry Caterpillar* (Carle, 1969) and holding the caterpillar puppet, pointed to the puppet and explained, "He got all the colors by eating all that stuff [the colors from the food]." In another instance, David and Marcus were both reading a big book about dinosaurs when Marcus said, "Dinosaurs eat grown ups." David replied, "No they don't. They eat grass." On another occasion, Victor and I were reading *Island Baby* (Keller, 1992), which is about a boy who lets a bird go that he has been caring for. At the end of the story, Victor asked, "What did the bird want to do?" He wanted to hear the bird's side of the story, which is not given in the text of the book.

I supported this strategy by encouraging children to discuss their books as they read and to model ways to think critically about books. Often, during our group reading time I asked the children "why" and "what if" questions, which helped the children think about other possibilities for how a story might come about if certain factors were changed. At the same time, some instances of this strategy ("He got all the colors by eating all that stuff [the colors from the food]") were hard to predict and hard to strengthen— they're just too much a part of children's inventiveness and creativity.

All of the starting off and in-text strategies, created by the children themselves and supported and nurtured by me, strengthened the children's literacy competence and social inclusion. On certain occasions, disputes between the children revealed their desire to make these intellectual and social bridges. Rikki, Liza, and Diana were each reading a book at the library table at Hawthorne, when Rikki suddenly started crying over her *Berenstain Bears* book.

LIZA: What'd she [Diana] do to hurt your feelings?
RIKKI: She [Diana] said I can't read.
LIZA: (turning to Diana) She [Rikki] knows how. Come on (gives Rikki a nudge toward the still open book. Rikki proceeds to make up a story as she turns the pages of the book. Liza listens, watches, and nods approvingly) You're readin. You're readin.

In this scene, Liza took the initiative (without my asking or assistance) in solving this dispute and helping Rikki. She sensed the depth of Rikki's hurt from the public perception that she couldn't do literacy like the others, and put Rikki back on track by giving her the peer encouragement she needed. This is an instance of developmentally and culturally responsive assistance *from a peer*—Liza responded to Rikki like an older sibling, problem solving with her and giving her the initial encouragement and maintaining a watchful eye as Rikki restarted her literacy performance of reading the book. And the verbal declaration, "You're readin. You're readin," which Liza said with some volume for others to hear, indicates Liza's knowledge that children themselves can bestow literacy competency and social inclusion on and for each other.

LEARNING MY ABCs

Marcus asked me to read *Chicka Chicka Boom Boom* with him. As I turned to the title page, Marcus stopped me and said, "Oh, I know how to read this. C, C, B, B." He pointed to each word in the title as he correctly identified the name of each initial letter.

After I wrote down her dictation, I asked Zariah if she knew how to write her name. She looked at me quizzically and asked, "My first ABCDs or my second ABCDs?" Zariah wanted to know whether I meant could she write her first name ("My first ABCDs") or her last name ("my second ABCDs"). She ended up writing both.

I asked Ronelle, after she finished her drawing, if she knew how to write her name. "Yes," she said. I asked her how she learned. "My mom taught me when I was three years old," she said. I asked her why. "So nobody would take my paper," Ronelle replied.

Marcus, Zariah, Ronelle, and most of their classmates expressed an interest in learning their "ABCs." The children are expressing this interest during the current debate in California (see, e.g., *Every Child a Reader*, 1995; *Teaching Reading*, 1996) and nationally (see, e.g., *Learning to Read and Write*, 1998; National Research Council, 1998; *The Unique Power of Reading*, 1998) on the role of alphabet identification and sound–symbol relationships in children's literacy development. When I started to teach these preschool children, I did not place much emphasis on alphabet-related activities. I wanted the children to have rich and interesting activities focused on children's literature and their own creative drawing and writing, and felt that alphabet activities would detract from this emphasis. Over time, though, as I got to know the teachers and the families, I began devoting more time to alphabet-related activities. I did so because such activities were valued by some teachers and many families, and because I learned to see the need for the children themselves to have the benefit of more attention to basic literacy skills. In short, I retained what I considered developmentally appropriate about my literacy teaching, while adding what I considered to be responsive to the needs and wishes of the teachers, children, and families.

Alphabet and Counting Books

I increased emphasis on skill development in two primary ways. First, I brought in alphabet books and incorporated name and letter writing into the children's journals and other writing and drawing projects. I embedded alphabet-related skills into quality children's literature and added activities that strengthened children's literary talents while creating opportunities for literary collaboration and social inclusion.

I read and shared such alphabet books as *26 Letters and 99 Cents* (Hoban, 1987), *K is for Kiss Goodnight* (Sardegna, 1994), *Chicka Chicka Boom Boom* (Martin & Archambault, 1989), and *The Calypso Alphabet* (Aagard, 1989). At the same time, I introduced and read such counting books as *Ten, Nine, Eight* (Bang, 1983), *Count!* (Fleming, 1992), and *Brian Wildsmith's 1, 2, 3's* (Wildsmith, 1965). With both kinds of books, I introduced the children to recognizing and discussing letters and numbers in playful, open-ended ways. In the spirit, too, of the children's interest in playing and improvising with oral and written language texts, I changed the books to become extensions and elaborations of the children's own experiences, wishes, and dreams. For instance, at the end of *K is for Kiss Goodnight* (Sardegna, 1994), I turned to the "A" page and reread the printed text, "A, all ready for bed," as "A, all ready for bed, but Kyeisha wants her mom to read to her." At the book's closing, which pictures the same girl fast asleep, I added, "And Kyeisha fell asleep and dreamed and dreamed of what she wanted to be when she grew up." Turning to the small group of children, I asked, "What do you all want to be when you grow up?"

CHARLES: A video store guy. Blockbusters.
TIFFANY: (incredulous) Don't you want to be Michael Jordan?
CARL: Me, too [that is, a video store guy].
ALICIA: A ballerina.
TIFFANY: A hairdresser.
MAKISHA: Me, too.
SARAH: Me, too.

Turning to the back of the book, which shows the complete alphabet, I asked the children to "point to or say your favorite letter." One child pointed randomly without identifying the letter and another said a letter, and then I had to help them find it, and the other five children wanted to find the letter that started their names. As the fourth child to choose a letter in our small group, Maria chose "A," but then Elena leaned over and told Maria in Spanish to choose the letter that started her name. I then asked Maria if she wanted to choose again, she said yes, and I helped her find "M."

I also played with the texts of the counting books. In *Ten, Nine, Eight* (Bang, 1983), the dedication page shows a man and a young child sitting together on a rocker, and I made up a new text.

DEDICATION: Kyeisha told her father: Daddy, tell me just one more
    story. (I told the children to gesture for one more story)
PAGE 1: (actual text: "10 small toes all washed and warm") OK, said
    Daddy. And he started to tell a story . . . once upon a time there was
    a little girl who was about to go to sleep, and her 10 toes were all
    lined up in a row. (the children and I then counted the toes in the
    illustration, "forward" from right to left and then "backward" from
    right to left to double-check, then counted to 10 on our fingers, and
    finally we counted all our feet as we sat cross-legged on the rug)
PAGE 2: (actual text: "9 soft friends in a quiet room") And all of the little
    girl's toys were about to go to sleep, too. (we then counted the girl's

animals, and I then passed the book around, asking the children to see if they could find the tiny mouse in the illustration)

PAGE 3: (actual text: "8 square windowpanes with falling snow") And as night continued, the snow began to fall. (we counted the window panes, and I asked the children to find the cat in the illustration. I asked the children how a stuffed animal cat could possibly get up and move around)

In this way, and in other stories and books, I modeled ways for the children to play with and manipulate a book's given text and story line. This gave the children a communal, small group experience in improvising text making and storytelling, and gave them ideas for their own book reading strategies. The *Ten, Nine, Eight* book remained a counting book, though, as we worked on such early numeracy skills as identifying the numeral on each page and counting the objects. In this companion process, I also guided the children in their beginning journey to gain greater competency in playing with varied levels of symbol use. By talking about the objects and characters in the book by name, we experienced the first-order or direct symbolism (Vygotsky, 1978) of playing with words and vocabulary ("cat," "mouse," "father," "Kyeisha"). By looking at and discussing the printed text and numerals and objects, we experienced the second-order symbolism (Vygotsky, 1978) of words and numbers representing real-life objects.

I also involved the children in touching and counting the objects and tracing the letters, and asked them to raise a clenched fist in celebration and recognition of the first letter of their own name, rather than asking the children to fill out worksheets practicing letter and numeral formation. These kinds of alphabet and number activities, which I embedded in children's literature and the children's interest in narrative and social collaboration, were developmentally appropriate because they were reasonable to expect the children to do. I also considered the activities child- and culturally responsive. The activities created opportunities for the children to bring their personal experiences and culturally influenced ways of talking and interacting to bear on their early literacy involvement, to promote group call-and-response scripts, to sing and clap along with the musicality and rhythm of language, and to emphasize here and there in selected and deliberate ways their interest (as influenced by adults) in learning literacy skills, tools, and strategies.

Sound–Symbol Correspondence

After she wrote several letters and her name in her journal, I asked Maya how she learned "to write her letters." "Nobody taught me," Maya replied. "I have a chart [of the alphabet] at home on my TV."

I asked Michael what he wanted to dictate for his journal drawing. "All I know is my letters," he said. "My dad is trying to teach me how to read and he's trying to teach me how to write a poem."

Ayanna picked up the wordless book *The Apple Bird* (Wildsmith, 1983) and looked through the pages. She turned to me and said, "Teacher, where's the stuff that you read?"

Maya, Michael, Ayanna, and many of their classmates expressed an interest in understanding sound–symbol correspondences and the role of letters and words in reading and writing. As I worked with the children and got to know their teachers and families, I also saw the need to increase the amount of attention that I devoted to sound–symbol activities. Slowly, and in small doses, I created a growing set of materials and activities focusing on letter recognition and corresponding sounds.

Sound–Symbol Strategies. I used a collection of sound–symbol (SS) strategies for guiding the children's experiences.

SS #1. Play games with the sight and sounds of words. For example, when we first gathered on the rug or at a table for our small group work, we clapped our hands in unison as we chanted the syllables of our names ("De-me-tri-us, De-me-tri-us, De-me-tri-us" and "Me-lis-sa, Me-lis-sa, Me-lis-sa"), going around the circle. In another activity, we played the I Spy game. I modeled the game for the children: "I spy a book cover on the wall that also starts with the same first sound as in *Spot*," or "I spy someone in our circle whose name begins with the same sound as the beginning of Mr. Meier." In another activity, we went on a "letter hunt" on a page of a big book. In *The Very Hungry Caterpillar*, we looked for the letters "c" or "v" and counted the letter totals for a particular page. We also counted the letter totals of the children's names that I had written on large laminated name tags (decorated with an animal sticker of their choice). We counted the longest and shortest names, and grouped the name tags by "names that start with S" and "names that start with M," and then counted the relative quantities of these groups.

SS #2: Introduce letter identification activities in playful ways. I used small alphabet flash cards with a single letter ("e") on one side and an animal (elephant) on the other. I selected a small number of the cards for animal and letter guessing as part of a memory game with small groups of children. I always went over the cards with the children first, and helped children who needed extra assistance. In another activity, I used a large alphabet flip chart with a picture of an animal (alligator, octopus, vicuña) and the accompanying initial letter ("Aa, Oo, Vv"). With the children, I always pointed first to the animal ("alligator, octopus, vicuña") and then to the letter ("Aa, Oo, Vv") as I waited a half-second for the children to fill in the correct animal and letter. I also made little stories out of the letter cards: for Tt/turtle, I said, "See, the turtle goes into her shell when she's scared." To which Dashawn once replied, "This is our [human] shell," as he tapped his chest.

In a third activity, I taught the children to raise a clenched fist and say their name out loud when they heard or saw the letter that started their own name. This often prompted the children to call out spontaneously the names of other children in their class whose names also started with that letter. I also added the gimmick of asking the children to close their eyes after "Z," and then flipping back to the "A" page as I said, "Now look where we are!" The children opened their eyes, and delighted in our return to the beginning of the alphabet. Some children, like Julio, quickly internalized this mini-routine. On one occasion, Julio read the entire chart of 26 letters to Ray, his audience of one. Starting with "A for alligator," Julio paused to look at me when he got stuck, and I supplied the letters for him. After he got to "Z," Julio announced (still only to Ray), "OK everybody, close your eyes," and as Ray closed his eyes Julio flipped back to the "A" page.

SS #3: Extend the children's oral language dictation. I framed and guided the children in their dictation after they drew and wrote. I asked the children if they knew how to write their names, and if they didn't, I often helped them either say the letters in their name or write the first letter or two. I broke the task down to make it manageable and not overly frustrating. I also invited the children to "read back" their dictated messages and texts. I read most of the children's text and stopped here and there in key places such as at the end of phrases and sentences to let the children supply the words. For example, I read, "I went to the park with my _____," and the child filled in "momma." I also used my finger to track my writing to show the children what we were reading together. Occasionally, children read back more than the missing word or two, remembering longer chunks of text or adding new phrases and sentences. I also provided the correct spellings for children who asked and who I thought would not be overwhelmed by the task. In these situations, I dictated the words letter by letter for the children, or worked with the children to guess the *simplest* sound–letter correspondences in their texts.

Playing with Dictation

Sarah was finishing up her dictation for her drawing when she announced, "Now my show is done!" Not all of the children ended their dictated texts with such drama, but almost all of the children enjoyed our dictation activities because they extended their language and literacy use in creative ways. The majority of the children did not dictate in the deliberate word-for-word and syllable-by-syllable style sometimes referred to as "dictation style" (for more on dictation, see Dyson, 1986; King & Rentel, 1981; McNamee, 1987; Paley, 1981; Sulzby, 1985, 1987). Rather, many of the children either dictated short texts as if they were simply conversing with me or created longer stories that resembled oral storytelling. By the end of a year working with each new class of children, though, some of the children slowed down their dictation and looked at the speed of my pen as I wrote. They were gauging the speed of their oral language compared with the speed of my written language, and starting to match oral and written language as it went from their minds to the paper.

For the children who spoke in long spurts of oral language, I wrote down as much as I could but did not stop their storytelling. I wanted them to gain the experience of watching me write at least some of their words and continue their story unhindered.

MR. MEIER: OK, Asia, ready for your dictation?

ASIA: Um, my always—my mommy always takes me to the park.

MR. MEIER: (writing) My . . .

ASIA: And she always—and she always takes me to the um, um, to the party and to the mov/and to the um, um, and to the/to my birthday cake and then, and then to my—and sh/I—we get to go, my brother goes to my/his school and I get to come over his school, if I'm five. But I'm gonna come to this school any more if I'm gonna stay with Steven, but Steven is huh . . .

MR. MEIER: How old, how old is Steven?

ASIA: Five. And then . . .

MR. MEIER: And is he in kindergarten now?

ASIA: Mmmm hmmm. Then he . . . and then my brother and my mommy and my daddy and me and and my frien/and my mommy's friend going to the party. I weared a pretty dress, but I didn't take it to school . . . and then my mom, my mom weared a dress. And my mommy and my brother weared a—

MR. MEIER: So you like to wear a dress?

ASIA: Mmmm hmmm. And then I couldn't took it to school because my mommy said no I can't. And then she said, and then she said now I can take my dress to school now if I, if I, if I, if I, if I, if I, if my mom don't bring it to school in a bag but if, if—if I do, if I—if my mom wears her dress then I wear my own dress and my, and my Steven wears his pants and his shirt, then then he wears that. And my mommy . . . and my, and my mommy, and my mommy went to another place. It was called, um, da um, the party station. But my mommy didn't catch cold there.

And Asia continued on with her story, stopping and pausing to see where her tale could continue and using the "um"s and staccato "if I"s to keep up the rhythm and the flow as she went.

Other children loved to interweave dialogue and narration, and mix in friends and family in their storytelling on paper. It was in this kind of flow of language that the children could flex their linguistic muscles and improvise as they went. After Mariah completed her customary journal entry of writing her name, her mother's name, and a few words she knew how to spell, she was ready for her dictation.

> I miss my cat. My momma and me are going to get a birthday cake. It's going to be on the 12th, 1996. I miss you [i.e., the cat]. We're going to see you next time. I know your daddy is waiting to see me. My momma said she's going to get me a bird. But if you want to come and see me, it's OK! Cat, I love you. If you want me to baby-sit you, I will.

Mariah creates an involved story using first person ("I miss my cat") and third person ("My momma said") and involving the characters of her cat, her mother, and a bird, as well as the possibility of a four-year-old baby-sitting a cat. Mariah also uses rich and varied syntax (from the simple declarative sentence, "I miss my cat," to the repetition of "if" condition-als, "If you want to come and see" and "If you want me to baby-sit you, I will"). In comparison with what the children were able to write, dicta-tion offered opportunities for Mariah and her classmates to frame oral language texts rich in character, plot, and dialogue.

I also took the children's dictation on the computer, which enabled me to write down more of the children's language and immediately print out multiple copies of the children's texts. Once I printed out their work, we read the dictated text together, and I asked the children to make an accompany-ing illustration. On one occasion, I asked the children to dictate something about what they liked to do at home, and I entitled their work, "All About Me." If needed, I gave dictation prompts such as, "What do you like to do at home?" "What do you like to do at school?" and "What is your favorite book?"

> At home, I like to play with my new horsies. With the pink and the purple. I run the horses. I feed them. Their names are Barbara and the other girl's name is Neesie. I also like to play with my other toys. I play in my room. And at school, I like to play in the doll corner and play with the baby dolls. I like to use the computers and read books. I like the Huggles books. The End
> —Mira

At home, I like to play with my toys. And I like to watch *Space Jam*. I like it when Michael Jordan's arm gets long. Then he shoots the basketball. I also like to ride my bike. I ride without training wheels. At school, I like to play in the doll corner. I play with the toys and the other kids. I like to use the computer because I like to do the games and the programs. I also like to listen to the stories. I like *The Ugly Duckling*. The End

—Patrick

The speed of the computer helped Mira and Patrick create longer and more cohesive texts. The computer also gave me more time to ask questions and prompt the children as they dictated. The children then enjoyed helping me press the print commands and watching for the printer to produce their oral text onto the written page.

DRAWING, WRITING, READING—PUTTING IT ALL TOGETHER

In early May, four-year-olds Tanya, Surinder, Janet, and three other children drew and wrote together in their journals. Tanya, who loved to talk and discuss her work and social experiences, also loved to draw and was eager to learn how to write and spell words. When she worked on a single journal entry, Tanya sometimes liked to draw only and not write, as depicted in Figure 4.1. On other occasions, Tanya liked to concentrate on her writing and not include a drawing. Not interested on that June day with drawing, Tanya went directly to writing, as depicted in Figure 4.2. Tanya wrote the top row of large letters by herself, changing colored markers as she went and carefully forming the letters. Although I did not ask, possibly these were random letters. But in looking at what happened next, it was more likely that Tanya used her writing *as her dictation*. In this way, Tanya created a hybrid dictation/writing, combining two different kinds of literacy activities.

After writing the big letters, Tanya indicated that she wanted to co-write a dictated text. On the first line of the smaller writing in the middle of the page, Tanya dictated, "I made." Knowing that Tanya was capable of problem solving possible sound–symbol correspondences with me, I asked Tanya for the letter in "I." As Tanya said, "I," she wrote it. I then repeated "made," and asked for the first letter in this word. Tanya said "m" and wrote "M" to the right of "I." I skipped the vowel "a" (I wanted her to concentrate on the consonants in this word), repeated "made," and asked Tanya for the letter that made the "d" sound. Tanya wasn't sure and so I told her. She wrote "d" to the right of the "M."

FIGURE 4.1. Tanya's Drawing

Tanya looked up from writing the "d" and said, "letters." Again, I wanted her to concentrate on listening for the consonants in "letters" (for more on children's sound–symbol understanding, see Bissex, 1980; Ferreiro & Teberosky, 1982; Graves, 1983). This worked well. Tanya identified the first letter in "letters," which she wrote backwards and upside down (and I didn't correct). I then helped Tanya identify the "t," "R," and "S." At this point, Tanya appeared tired and stopped (her version of a "developmentally appropriate pause"). Tanya then wrote a random second row of "SRPOSY" without my assistance. She read this line back as, "They're (that is, her top line of big letters) pretty." Then, in another incremental step of self-scaffolding, Tanya changed directions in her text and wrote "MOM" and then drew a heart to the right.

Then, gaining newfound energy, Tanya wanted to spell "cat" and "dog," but told me that she didn't know how to write the words. Without

FIGURE 4.2. Tanya's Dictation and Writing

waiting for my help, Tanya left the table and took her journal over to the alphabet chart on a wall across the room. Tanya copied down "cat" and "dog" from the "c" and "d" alphabet panels. In Figure 4.2, "cat" is written on the last row, to the left, and the "a" is nestled inside the "C." "Dog" is written to the right, the "d" written as a reversal.

How did Tanya put her literacy talents and skills together in her hybrid dictation/writing activity? Tanya directed the order and timeline of her own work. She started with a line of random letters, which she easily wrote as she played with making the letters in different colors. Tanya and I then worked on our collaborative sound–symbol relationships, which was hard work, and Tanya invested a great deal of concentration in this challenge. It was helpful for Tanya to enlist my assistance in this effort. Getting tired, Tanya then wrote a word she knew by heart ("mom") before copying words ("cat" and "dog") from the alphabet chart. In this way, Tanya started with independent work (the big letters), then engaged in collaborative work (sound–symbol writing), and then, having crested this challenging hill, self-scaffolded and problem solved the rest (writing "mom," "cat," "dog") on her own.

During the challenging middle portion of her work, I could have insisted that I write the dictation as Tanya spoke. This could be seen as more developmentally appropriate for her, but I knew Tanya and understood her desire (and her mother's, since I had taught Tanya's older sister in kindergarten) to propel *her own* literacy development. In the moments of writing the dictation with me, it also meant a lot to Tanya to have a greater sense of public control over the dictation than if I had done all the writing and she had done only the talking. In this way, Tanya tries to place literacy within the center of her school identity, hoping that school literacy is "true" to her "real self" (Willis, 1995, p. 33) and also at the same time (by working with me) to her "teacher and audience of readers who are in effect, evaluating" her "culture, thinking, language, and reality" (Willis, 1995, p. 33). Also, Tanya works to expand her own zone of proximal development (Bruner, 1986; Vygotsky, 1978, 1986) in terms of her control over letters, sounds, a message, the entire journal activity, and the possibilities for social interaction that will help her move along in her journey toward greater social inclusion and school literacy competency. Tanya plays at an important early juncture along the two potentially divergent paths of developmental literacy learning and the diversity of children's interests in getting bigger and learning to do literacy.

Janet was another child who loved to draw and could write several words, as depicted in Figure 4.3. As I sat next to Janet on that day in early June, she also wanted to write her dictation, as shown in Figure 4.4. After I finished helping Tanya with her writing, I had time to work with Janet. Janet had drawn a large human figure on the left side of the page and then wanted to do her dictation. Janet wanted her dictation/writing to say, "He's got chicken pox." Since I knew that Janet could write a few words on her own and loved to spell (and we were running short on time and I needed to help the other children), I spelled the words for Janet and she wrote them. I told Janet the consonants and the vowels because I knew that she could write most of the letters of the alphabet on her own. So we worked together, as I supplied the correct letters and Janet wrote them down. In effect, I did the dictation and Janet did the writing. Janet wrote "HESGOT" on the bottom line and then "CHICKE" on the next line above, before finally writing "MPOX" (she wrote an "M" instead of an "N") on the top line. Why did Janet write from the bottom up? Possibly, she was so used to my writing the children's dictation at the bottom of the page that she followed my modeling.

I thought Janet was tired and done, but she wanted to continue. Turning to the next page in her journal, she revealed another large figure, as

FIGURE 4.3. Janet's Drawing and Writing

shown in Figure 4.5. "He's got long hair," Janet wanted as her text. I followed the same process of supplying the letters, which Janet wrote down. As she started to write "HES," Janet asked me, "The same as the other one?" referring to the "HES" that she wrote on the previous page. I nodded. So Janet turned back to that page, and went back and forth copying down the three letters in "HES." I then told her the remaining letters for "GOT LONG HAIR." On this page, as opposed to her earlier writing, Janet started her sentence higher up and wrote across and down the paper. Interested in writing her own letters and words, and knowledgeable about letter writing, Janet was able to carry out her own dictation by writing the correct letters that I supplied. Janet also helped the process along by drawing one large human figure, keeping her dictated sentences simple ("He's got

FIGURE 4.4. Janet's Chicken Pox Drawing and Writing

chicken pox" and "He's got long hair"), and starting each sentence with the same word ("HES").

I then moved over to work with Surinder, who spoke Hindi and had a beginning command of English. Surinder had drawn an Edvard Munch-like array of human faces, as shown in Figure 4.6. Surinder created a montage of drawn faces and dictated family names that can be read in any direction and from any starting point. Starting with the central picture later dictated as "me," Surinder named his "mom" (drawn in pink magic marker), "my friend," "dad," "grandma," "sister," "her mom (of pink mom above)," "baby," "other friend," "baby," and "sister." Surinder combined the power of gesture and the concrete by pointing to each of the faces, which represented partly his real family and partly a collection of possible family and friend connections, and then making them come alive with a dictated label of "me" or "mom" or "sister." Surinder's process of one-to-one correspondence of a verbal family label for each unnamed face shows a different developmental path from the writing of Tanya and Janet, who worked to match letter sounds with written alphabetic symbols. Still learning English, Surinder

FIGURE 4.5. Janet's Long Hair Drawing and Writing

was more interested in short English labels grouped around the common theme of family as his way of successfully doing the journal activity.

Tanya, Janet, and Surinder reveal a mini-portrait of possible ways for children to learn how to put together letters and sounds and pictures. Tanya goes back and forth between writing known words and learning new ways of writing. Janet extends her skills in writing through her knowledge of letter names and writing. Surinder plays with the creativity of drawn representations and verbal-to-print labels. His verbal labels, though, are really more; they too tell a mini-story just as do Tanya's and Janet's texts. Surinder informs his work by combining and orchestrating what he can draw (human faces), his world experience (family and friends), and his knowledge of a new language (family and friend words). It is this kind of in-the-moment integration of symbol and sense and experience that encourages Surinder to play with literacy and literary expression in school.

Tanya, Janet, Surinder. As they gather around the same table in their classroom, the early history of their oral and written language work un-

FIGURE 4.6. Surinder's Family Drawing and Dictation

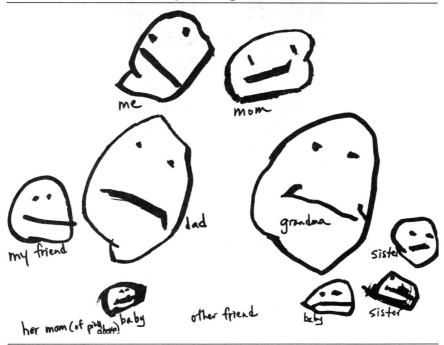

folds according to their interests and talents. I act as guide and interpreter, helping the children to rely on their current knowledge and skills and to extend themselves in ways that are not frustrating and overwhelming. In playing with the children's zones of proximal development (Vygotsky, 1978, 1986), I learn to see and hear how the children manipulate symbols according to their varied interests and skills. It is in the resulting teaching–learning mix of closely working with Janet to identify the first letter in "made" and writing "her mom (of pink mom above)" for Surinder that the children and I get to know each other's literary histories-in-the-making. And in this process, tensions of literacy form and function propel the children in their literacy, encouraging them to follow their own developmental paths within responsive teaching environments.

Chapter 5

A Contemporary Childhood–
Literacy in a Child's World

Is black in the rainbow?

–Carl

Ronnie, Joseph, and Janet were drawing in their journals and talking about Power Rangers.

RONNIE: These are the Power Rangers. My favorite Power Ranger is green.
JOSEPH: (to Ronnie) Draw the black. The black one is my favorite.
(Ronnie draws a black Power Ranger)
RONNIE: My favorite Power Ranger is green. The black is for Joseph.
(draws a red Ranger and turns to Janet) Janet is the red one.

For Carl ("Is black in the rainbow?"), and Janet, Ronnie, and Joseph ("Draw the black. The black one is my favorite"), occasions for literacy that speak to children's identities and interests make room for the diversity of children's orientations toward literacy in our contemporary schools.

TEXTS AND GENRES—TOWARD A PLAYFUL MIX

Creating new kinds of texts and genres provided a powerful motivation for the children to gather around books and work with smelly magic markers and paper. On one occasion, I worked with Larry, Juan, and Ray as they talked and drew in their journals.

LARRY: (to Juan) What you drawing?
JUAN: My mom.
RAY: How you like mine, Mr. Meier? (I smile and nod)
LARRY: It's a Power Ranger Mezzoid. Juan, your mom is pretty.
JUAN: (holding marker) This smells like Coca Cola. (to Larry) Look at my mommy. It turns into a monster.

LARRY: In your dream?
JUAN: No, my mommy's outside.
LARRY: How'd she turn into a monster?
JUAN: I'm just playing.

In Juan's explanation, "I'm just playing," to Larry, Juan spins out a double tale—the one that he draws and the other that he tells. Juan, a Spanish speaker who loved to use playful conversations with peers to gain fluency in English, plays his drawn journal page and the oral conversation off each other in order to see where this dialogical process takes him. Starting out with his drawing, Juan probably did not know where the magic marker would take him. Juan's "I'm just playing" is the language that changes his drawing into whatever he wants it to be, and then back again if he wants, connecting himself with Larry and with the continual inventiveness of his journal page. It is through the active use of language to engage the other—both the other of the represented page and the other in form of his peer, Larry—that Juan helps himself along in the developmental journey of playing with language, thought, and interaction.

By talking and drawing with each other, the children enact a dynamic and dialogical process of going back and forth between language, symbols, and discourse (Bakhtin, 1981, 1986). By playing with the journal page and by playing with language, Juan and the other children experiment with interpreting and creating genres (Bakhtin, 1981, 1986), which are the "intimate genres and styles" from home and literature based on "maximum internal proximity of the speaker and addressee" (Bakhtin, 1986, p. 97). The children's own personal genres are based on the content and form of their drawings and writing. In creating these genres, the children experiment with new literary forms and content that suit the intellectual and social demands of the moment, and also fit their "ways with words" (Heath, 1983) from home and community.

In learning to create their own genres, the children find themselves in a quandary: They are just learning to recognize and replicate traditional literary conventions and forms such as fairy tales and dictation and oral storytelling, and also are just learning to orchestrate the very literary talents and skills needed to create these forms and genres. So what do children do with this challenge? They mess about in a middle ground between the conventional genres and literary forms to be learned in school and the more personal forms and uses of language learned from home and community. For example, in learning to do dictation, the children need to make sense of the genre of dictation as I present it, and also to bring in their personal interests (family, friends, themselves) and literary talents (storytelling, language as performance, basic skills) to the task.

When I first started dictation with the children, I asked them to "tell me something about your drawing or anything else you want to write." The children often gave me a quizzical look as if to say, "Mr. Meier, why do I need to add something more? What's wrong with just talking about it—my drawing speaks for itself." Over time, as I introduced additional dictation strategies and opportunities, the children learned to see more possibilities for enhancing the quality of their work and our social interaction.

In early March at Hawthorne Preschool, I worked with Niasha, Anthony, Abdul, Jordan, Mia, and Lynne. I wanted them to draw on a small piece of paper and dictate something they liked to do. I first showed them work from a previous group.

MR. MEIER: This is what the kids did the other day. (I show Justin's drawing and read his dictated text) "I like to play Power Rangers. The pink one is my favorite. I'd like to be a Power Ranger. Justin." And this is Monique's. "I like to color and draw. I like to draw with pink and yellow. Monique." And this is Jimmy's. "I like to go to school. I like to play. At home I run around my house." How many of you want to use the people crayons [crayons matching a range of human skin hues]?
CHILDREN: I do (a few children).
MR. MEIER: OK. I'll put them out and I also have markers.

The children settled in to draw and talk together. Abdul drew a square and then several other shapes.

MR. MEIER: You all done, Abdul?
ABDUL: (to me) What are you gonna do? Write our names?
ANTHONY: Yeah.
MR. MEIER: OK Abdul. Let's do your dictation. What do you like to do? Here, you sit . . .
JORDON: I'm gonna write my name.
MR. MEIER: What do you like to do?
ABDUL: I like to play. I like to play basketball. I like to play volleyball. I like to go to a . . . I like to play with my mom. I like to go to my daddy's house.
JORDON: (to me) You not talking? Why you not talking any, Mr. Meier?
ABDUL: Hey.
JORDON: Mr. Meier, why you not talking?
MR. MEIER: I was thinking about it. "I like to play with my mom."
ABDUL: (adding to his text as I continue writing) I like to go to the beach.
ANTHONY: . . . the beach.

MIA: Look it, Mr. Meier. (shows her drawing)
ANTHONY: I go to the beach, too. I go to all beach. I go swimming.
   Today . . . my mom say I go swimming.
MIA: I go swimming today, too.

My desire to have the children add oral/written language texts to their drawings and writings adds another layer of literacy to their jointly enacted literary and social experience. In this scene, Abdul has the idea (like some of his classmates) that when I say "dictation" it means I will write down their names, which I do for the children who have a difficult time writing their names. I usually do the name writing after the message because I want the children to have the immediacy of first connecting their oral language texts with their writing and artwork. I also repeat the children's oral language as I write; since I did not do that here, Jordan notices the change in routine and asks, "Mr. Meier, why you not talking?"

In teaching dictation as a literacy genre in school, I ask the children to mix their linguistic and personal talents and skills with my particular dictation format. The children, in turn, understand the dictation genre in their own particular ways. For instance, Abdul ("What are you gonna do? Write our names?") focuses on one aspect of the dictation activity—the name writing. Jordan ("I'm gonna write my name" and "Why you not talking any, Mr. Meier?") has a more complete idea of the entire dictation activity as I have constructed it. Abdul and Jordan are in different developmental places in recognizing and coordinating the layers of language and experience in this activity. If all our literacy activities and the parameters for successful participation targeted only Jordan, Abdul would not feel included and competent. Abdul and some of the other children need, then, extended opportunities to talk and socialize that become comfortable stepping stones for understanding school-based literacy genres. And along the way, although the children's discussion of the suddenly popular topic of the beach (as Abdul starts a chain of beach comments) does not appear in their final literary products, their talk and socializing provide a mixing ground for strengthening their interests in each other, outside experiences, and the literacy task at hand. Their discussion encourages the children's "words" to "belong" (Bakhtin, 1986, p. 85) to them and to the common, shared task of dictation.

MEDIA AND POPULAR CULTURE—SPRINGBOARDS TO LITERACY

The media and popular culture, which are powerful influences on children's interests and friendships, also influenced the children's social interest in literacy.

MR. MEIER: (holding up the "Xx" page on the large alphabet flip chart)
    And this is . . .
DEMETRA: "X," for ex-girlfriend.
MR. MEIER: How'd you learn that?
TAMMY: People *been* knowing that! From Ricki Lake [popular television
    talk show].

It is a challenge for teachers, educators, and parents to acknowledge and
make a place for children's interests in popular culture, and to let them
influence children's efforts to engage with literacy in schools. While elements of contemporary media culture do promote the attraction of violence
(Levin, 1998) and the continuation of racial and gender stereotypes, and
these are to be avoided, making room for certain elements of popular culture can provide a common pool of experience for literacy conversation,
representation, and performance. The children's references to popular
culture also strengthened the quality of addressivity (Bakhtin, 1986) among
the children; the shared set of references to popular movies and games
heightened the children's interest in each other and supplied shared content for their literacy experiences.

    When I read a book about a group of monkeys who help a lion cross a
river and then trick the lion into falling into the river, the children and I
debated the fairness of this trick.

MR. MEIER: Do you think it was fair for the monkeys to trick the lion
    into falling into the water?
CHILDREN: No, not really.
MR. MEIER: Who's seen *The Lion King* [movie]? (all the children raise
    their hands) Do you think it was right for Scar and Mustafa to fight?
EMERALD: They fought and one of them got killed.
DANTE: Yeah, he died. He fell off the cliff.
MR. MEIER: In this book, did the lion do anything to the monkeys?
    (children shake their heads) Did Mustafa do anything to Scar?
DANTE: No.

Using the common shared experience of *The Lion King* movie, the children
can use the movie's events and characters to begin reflecting and thinking
about issues of violence and morality in school-based literacy activities. Not
only does *The Lion King* provide a shared out-of-school experience for the
children, but it provides a narrative and complicated set of human/ani-
mal conflicts involving power and control in family life. By referring to the
movie, we can use a popular media story as a springboard into our literacy
activity.

In late January, Keith, Lamile, Ricky, Kysha, and Chantal worked in their journals at Hawthorne.

KEITH: Mr. Meier, look at mines. I know how to draw a triangle. (draws a triangle) Look at mines, Mr. Meier.
RICKY: (drawing a human figure) That's me going crazy.
KYSHA: (drawing large blocks of color right next to each other, and pointing to certain colors as she turns to Chantal) This is John Smith and this is Pocahontas.
CHANTAL: No, the black one is John Smith and the pink one is Pocahontas.
MR. MEIER: OK, Kysha, ready for your dictation?
KYSHA: OK. This (black) is John Smith and this (pink) is Pocahontas. This (blue) is her mother and this (yellow) is her father and this (green) is her grandma.

Using large swatches of color on her paper, and no attempts at representation of human figures, Kysha created a drawing that might be interpreted as deliberate scribble scrabble. Yet, given the discussion that occurred with Chantal and Kysha's dictation with me, Kysha's final literary work depicts the movie's poignant ties and separations of family and friendship. Something about *Pocahontas* spoke powerfully to Kysha and her friends, and something about the push-pull of John Smith and Pocahontas's family attracted Kysha to create a four-year-old's version of a sociogram. The movie, as recreated and reinterpreted in the children's literacy activity, serves as an important narrative for Kysha about the bonds of family and about the experience of life and people beyond these boundaries and experiences. As the children and I made use of the movie *The Lion King* in discussing the tricking of the lion by the monkeys in the book, so does the movie *Pocahontas* serve as a social and literacy bridge to friends (Chantal), to out-of-school experiences (popular movies), and to school literacy experiences.

FRIENDS AND FAMILY—MAKING CONNECTIONS TO TEXTS

While the children used heroes and heroines from movies and television for their literacy content, the children's most significant characters and plots came from their families and friends. For instance, the children could always rely on their families for the content of their dictation.

MELVIN: I want to be Superbird. I want to be a superhero. I want to go to painting on paper with my dad. I want to go on Saturday.

ANNA: My daddy took me to Chuck E Cheese. He got me a sticker and
    put it on my face. I hugged Mickey Mouse.
ALEXIS: I made me a cute picture for my momma.

Friends and family are powerful partners in enticing the children to engage
in literacy activities and promote a sense of social inclusion and literacy competency. Sisters, brothers, moms and dads, grandmas and grandpas, aunties
and uncles, cousins, and neighbors all provide a large supporting cast of real-
life characters for the children to bring to literacy. Whether the children were
seated together on the rug for a story or talking and working at a table, their
talk and interweaving of family and friends promoted literacy engagement
founded upon their funds of knowledge (Moll, Amanti, Neff, & Gonzalez,
1992) or their life experiences and information about everyday activities.
Further, opportunities for the children to include their families in the content of their literacy work promoted a sense of the children "as members of
extended families" (Ladson-Billings, 1994, p. 76) in school.

One day in the middle of April, Tawana and Ashayah drew and wrote
in their journals as they sat side by side at a table. Tawana, somewhat
quiet in nature, and Ashayah, more vocal and independent, were friends.
On her page, Ashayah wrote "BOOK," then her first and last name, then
"DOG," "CAT," "PIG," and her mother's first name, and then a large picture of flowers and a sun. After Ashayah wrote "BOOK" and the first
few words, Tawana became interested in Ashayah's writing. She asked
Ashayah to help her spell some words. Ashayah told Tawana how to write
the letters for "BOOK," which Tawana wrote by herself in the same upper
left-hand corner of the page. Tawana then went on to write a "B," a "D,"
and an "A." She also wrote her name on her own. Tawana finished by
writing rows of "R"s and various other letters.

MR. MEIER: OK, great, Tawana. Let's do your dictation.
TAWANA: (as I started to write) This is my whole family. That's it.
MR. MEIER: OK. Ashayah, what do you want for your dictation?
ASHAYAH: (as I started to write) I worked with Tawana. We made
    happy books. We are the best of friends. We had—(self-corrects) we
    was working with Mr. Meier. Me and Tawana, we are best friends
    with Kia. She is Tawana cousin. Tawana, she's going to come over
    to my house.

Here, structured possibilities for children to work together in open-ended
literacy activities promote the kind of scaffolding assistance that expands
children's zones of proximal development (Vygotsky, 1978, 1986). Based
on their friendship, Ashayah helps Tawana learn how to spell and write

the letters for "BOOK." Ashayah assists Tawana in replicating the same word in the same place as on her own page. With both children sitting next to each other and doing the same literacy task, Ashayah's writing ("BOOK," then her first and last name, then "DOG," "CAT," "PIG") provides an immediate model to inspire Tawana to ask for Ashayah's help. The model and Ashayah's subsequent assistance make both developmental and responsive sense; the model initially allows Tawana to see what a peer is capable of writing, and then the assistance turns Tawana into an active learner and Ashayah into a guiding teacher.

This kind of peer-to-peer scaffolding also heightens the sense of addressivity between Ashayah and Tawana as friends and literacy collaborators. Tawana provides just the right amount of initiative taking (asking Ashayah to write "BOOK"), and Ashayah provides just the right amount of teaching (telling Tawana how to spell and write "BOOK"). This provided the feeling of success and confidence that Tawana apparently needed; after writing "BOOK," Tawana went on to write her name and write more letters. Ashayah also used her own dictation to recap the activity and put into words (for all to hear) how literacy can help strengthen friendships and kinship ties in and out of the classroom ("I worked with Tawana. We made happy books. We are the best of friends").

In another scene, Gerardo worked in his journal alongside Manuel and four other children. As they often did, Gerardo and Manuel started their journal work by alternately drawing and smelling the magic markers.

GERARDO: (to Manuel) Make yours [drawing] smell pretty.
MANUEL: I like yours [drawing].
GERARDO: Give me your marker. (draws the same rounded shape on Manuel's paper) Here, I made you a dinosaur. It's cool. So be cool.
MANUEL: Can you make me a TV?
GERARDO: Sure. (draws a box)
MANUEL: Make me a man now here. (draws an elaborate figure)
GERARDO: I made you a man, but I made you a vampire!

Just as Tawana asks Ashayah for help, which she provides with a sense of developmental and personal responsiveness, Gerardo and Manuel enact a similar process of child initiating (Manuel: "Can you make me a TV?"), peer-to-peer scaffolding (Gerardo: "Here, I made you a dinosaur") and responding to each other's talents and skills (Manuel: "I like yours"). In addition, the children use the kid lingo and syntax of contemporary childhood (Gerardo: "Here, I made you a dinosaur. It's cool. So be cool") to solidify their social cohesion and literacy collaboration. Further, in a process of literary inventiveness and playfulness that fortifies social inclusion (similar to Larry's "How'd she turn into a monster?" and Juan's "I'm just playing"), Manuel and Gerardo also play with their literary creations (Gerardo: "I made you a man, but I made you a vampire!").

The books that I read to the children also provided opportunities for the children to bring in their friends and families. *In Daddy's Arms I Am Tall: African Americans Celebrating Fathers* (Steptoe, 1997) is a collection of proverbs and poems set against artwork of varied media. Although the text is sophisticated, the children loved the artwork and the powerful images of African American fathers and their families. In telling a new text, I combined what made sense developmentally with the power of cultural responsiveness in the artwork and messages, and emphasized the children's participation with all members of their immediate and extended families.

MR. MEIER: (reading the title to Rajiv, Michele, Dennis, Montel, Abdul, Malcolm, and Paris) "In Daddy's Arms I Am Tall." Reach your arms way up high. (children and I stretch toward the ceiling; I then open to the first page depicting a father walking to the Ashanti proverb, "When you follow in the path of your father, you learn to walk like him") My father takes big big big steps. (the children and I move our hands in big steps) And sometimes (as I turn the page to a poem, "In Daddy's Arms" by Folami Abiade) I hug my daddy and he hugs me. (the children and I give ourselves a hug) And on Sundays (as I turn to the next page and a poem entitled "Her Daddy's Hands" by Angela Johnson) my daddy and my mommy go to . . .
CHILDREN: church. (the man and woman in the illustration are dressed in a suit and fancy white dress and hat)
MR. MEIER: . . . and they walk hand in hand. (the page has a large inset picture of the couple holding hands)

I continued on with the new text as we acted out the movement of the artwork. When we came to a poem entitled "Lightning Jumpshot" by Michael Burgess, and the artwork showing a basketball and a court, Abdul blurted out, "I slam dunk with my dad."

In closing the book, I asked the children what they liked to do with their families.

MONTEL: My dad takes me to Chuck E Cheese to play the games. I play Play Station at home. Santa Claus got me a Play Station.
RAJIV: I like trains and cars. I play by myself.

PARIS: I like to go to Chuck E Cheese and play with my mommy.
DENNIS: My mom takes me to Chuck E Cheese and we eat pizza. We
    play on the slide.
ABDUL: I like to go to Disneyland with my family. I like to play with my
    car.
MICHELE: I like to go outside and play with my bike. I play by myself.

In the accompanying drawing and dictation activity, I again asked Abdul
what he liked to do with his family. He said:

> I like to play basketball with my dad. I like it when he picks me up
> and takes me somewhere. I like it when he picked me up when I
> was a baby.

For Michele's dictation, I again asked her what she liked to do with her
family.

> I like to go to grandma's house and eat. My brother, he eats
> breakfast pancakes. And I like to play with my little brother. I like
> to go to my grandma's house and she teaches me how to write my
> name.

Slam dunking, Chuck E Cheese, eating, writing names. Mothers, fathers,
grandmas, little brothers. The varied constellations of family and friends
provide the children with familiar out-of-school experiences for their literary conversations and activities. These connections also heighten the
sense of addressivity (Bakhtin, 1986) of the children's turning to our
texts—as Abdul looked at the picture of the basketball and court in *In
Daddy's Arms I Am Tall*, he couldn't help the spontaneous, "I slam dunk
with my dad." Slam dunking with dad and other family members is a
powerful image of family kinship, cultural identity, and personal power.
    This kind of home–school and child–family link is most relevant and
powerful when based on children's day-to-day life experiences. I read
Jonathan and His Mommy (Smalls, 1992) with the children, and we acted out
the ways that Jonathan and his mother walk together. As Jonathan and his
mommy take "big giant steps" and "talk in loud giant voices," so did we.
As Jonathan and his mommy take "bunny steps, hop-hop hop-hop-hop
(hip-hop, too, sometimes)," we did, too. As Jonathan and his mommy get
onto their "toes and do ballet steps, ballet steps, arms in the air," so did
we. The children delighted in the variations of movement of Jonathan and
his mommy, and loved the chance to act out the gestures and anticipate

how their walk would end. After we finished the book, I asked the children to read independently while I worked with one child at a time to dictate "how they liked to take a walk with their families." I wrote the children's comments on a long, one-foot wide roll of paper, which allowed the children to hear previous comments from their peers.

ABDUL: I run super fast!
TRACHELLE: I walk with no shoes.
SURINDER: I walk slow.
MONICA: I walk slow with my mommy.
ROBERT: I walk slow with my grandma.
CAROLYN: I like to hop.
SONYA: I like to hop with a ball.
CHERI: You got to hold hands.
CHERYL: (Cheri's twin sister) I hold hands with my mommy.
FRANCISCO: I like to walk like a rabbit.
RON: I like to walk to Blockbuster.
DEVON: I like to do criss-cross.
JOHN: Maybe all the way down the street.
LUPITA: I walk with my family.
MARVIN: Look both ways and run and walk.
JOSEPH: I run with Anthony [his big brother]. He's always winning me.
FAITH: I get on my dad's neck.
THUY: I like to zigzag.

Walking to Blockbuster, hopping with a ball, looking both ways and holding hands, getting on daddy's neck. The daily activity of walking is rendered varied and personal, tied to the children's interests and to their families and friends. *Jonathan and His Mommy* provides a shared in-school literacy focus, while the children's family experiences and ties provide the out-of-school content for adding words and images to our oral and written language work.

From self to family and back again. The children's connections to the books reveal their own personal, individual journeys toward independence, competency, and identity. Their connections, too, to their families and friends reveal the power of others to influence children's individual growth and serve as audience and mirror for children's literacy development. While walking on her "dad's neck," Faith does her own walk and walks with the help of her father. The big steps and the height of her father make her taller and faster, and yet they become her steps and her height, too. Their walk goes together, melding children's eagerness to grow and develop with adults' potential to lead and guide children.

GETTING BIGGER, GETTING SMARTER—
LITERACY IN PRESCHOOL AND KINDERGARTEN

Children starting out with the stuff of school literacy often want to play above their heads. Since "in play, it is as if he were a head taller than himself" (Vygotsky, 1978, p. 102), the children play with literacy tools and symbols to get bigger and get smarter in their journey toward literacy competency and social inclusion at home and school. For many of the children with whom I worked, getting bigger and getting smarter meant playing at being a big kid, acting and talking like their older siblings and relatives, and in general showing that they could do things with literacy beyond their supposed developmental levels.

One day, I watched Dalisa and Sonya during independent book sharing.

DALISA: (sitting in the chair and about to read teacher-style to Sonya)
    I'm gonna read this book.
SONYA: Don't read me nothing 'cause I don't want to be no kid.

Sonya expresses a desire to play at literacy "as if she were a head taller than herself" (Vygotsky, 1978, p. 102)—being read to by Dalisa would indicate to herself and publicly to others that she couldn't read on her own. In her desire for independence in literacy competence, Sonya wants to experience literacy on her own—to read and not be read to—ahead of any apparent developmental level of language arts development. From her warning to Dalisa ("Don't read me nothing 'cause I don't want to be no kid"), Sonya indicates her desire to go beyond her zone of proximal development (Vygotsky, 1978, 1986) for her literacy development *and* the perceptions of classmates regarding what she can and can't do with literacy. Sonya provides a cautionary reminder that language play, social interaction, and peer-to-peer scaffolding are not always beneficial for children, and especially so for those children like Sonya who want the personal satisfaction of accomplishing literacy learning on their own terms.

Sonya expresses her lack of interest in literacy learning through social interaction by her emphatic multiple negation ("don't," "nothing," "don't," "no") and the public assertion that she's beyond playing at being read to. Her social and public declaration to Dalisa (and everyone else in earshot) reveals a desire to do literacy in bigger and better ways. For Sonya and the other children, what it *appears* that you do with literacy can be as important as what you actually do. Being read to by Dalisa, then, could be interpreted by others as symbolic of a lack of literacy competency and social independence.

In this desire to *at least be seen* as more grown-up and competent, Sonya and many of her classmates pursue their own child development agenda for language arts learning. They are determined that their literacy learning be a big slice of the total portrait of themselves as increasingly more powerful thinkers and competent social participants in school.

Alphabet learning plays a prominent role in this desire to get bigger and get smarter. Ashayah, who helped Tawana earlier, was especially eager to explore alphabet-related activities.

MR. MEIER: Ashayah, did you ask your mom to write the words ["cat," "dog," "book" that she wrote in her journal], or did your mom say that she wanted you to learn them?
ASHAYAH: I did. I asked my mom to teach me how to spell them.
MR. MEIER: How come?
ASHAYAH: I want to be smart.

Ashayah reveals how children are able to enlist the help and assistance of adults and more capable peers (Vygotsky, 1978), and engage them in a process of acquiring literacy skills and furthering their own literacy interests. In the process, the children play upon and use their growing "funds of knowledge" (Moll et al., 1992) from family and friends to get ahead in their literacy development. Ashayah also reveals the value of providing children with the indicators and symbols of literacy achievement that make good developmental sense. In this way, the concrete markers and hands-on artifacts of literacy learning and achievement become recognizable as such by the children. For instance, Tawana needs to see and hear Ashayah help her write "BOOK." Manuel needs to see Gerardo draw a dinosaur and a TV for him. Since Tawana and Manuel like to learn from their friends, they need consistent opportunities to cultivate this kind of literacy learning and growth in an educational setting. And over time, the children need the accumulation of these concrete experiences and small moments of learning as public and private affirmation of their literacy success and school achievement.

Ashayah's comment, "I want to be smart," also indicates another layer of literacy intentions and interests. Ashayah and her peers are eager to do well and be "smart" as defined by friends, teachers, themselves, and families. The inner drive to do well in school at a young age propels Ashayah and her classmates to seek out the currency or the standards for doing well in school—and early on they see literacy, often characterized as learning the ABCs and spelling words and writing their names, as the foundation for school literacy learning.

As I spoke with the four- and five-year-old children, their perspectives about their upcoming kindergarten experience revealed the strong connection among literacy skills, appropriate social behavior, and school success. Based on expectations from families and teachers and the experiences of older siblings and relatives, kindergarten symbolized a major change in the children's literacy education and school participation. One summer, I talked with the children about their hopes and expectations for entering kindergarten.

MR. MEIER: What do you want to learn next year in kindergarten?

MARQUIS: I want to do my homework and be good on my homework. I want to listen to my kindergarten teacher.

DEMARIO: I'm gonna learn about rainbows and it's going to be nice kids and they're going to be talkin' to me and playing ball outside and that's all.

CARLOS: I want to learn how to spell my name and how to read and do my colors and do my alphabets and learn how to say my shapes and that's it.

TAMMY: I want to learn my name and my last name. My mommy's going to buy me a Barbie watch for kindergarten.

JOHN: I want to learn writing, the alphabets, letters, and all that pretty stuff in kindergarten.

DEMETRA: I want to learn my ABCs. I want to learn how to write my homework.

TIA: You can't scribble scrabble in kindergarten. You can in preschool. One time, I scribble scrabbled at my sister's house, and someone made fun of my picture.

ARTHUR: I'm going to play basketball and I'm going to be too busy doing work.

SURINDER: I'll listen to the teacher. I'll do projects.

MAKISHA: I want to learn my alphabets and my numbers and my colors. My name—my cousin and my sister tellin' me I write my name chicken scratch. But I don't.

Kindergarten embodies a new kind of literacy and behavioral experience that the children somehow know and yet somehow don't know. They have an idea that it is a chance to learn new literacy skills ("I want to learn how to spell my name") and new social experiences ("It's going to be nice kids and they're going to be talkin' to me"). The children sense, too, that what they have been doing and learning in preschool over the past 2 years is preparation for kindergarten. From their comments, the children expect kindergarten to be preschool and more—you can have friends and play, but you also will have homework and spend time working on the alphabet and [learning] "all that pretty stuff in kindergarten." Kindergarten is also a future experience and place for the children to join their big brothers and sisters, and have more powerful learning opportunities for getting bigger and getting smarter. It is a place where Makisha can "learn my alphabets and my numbers and my colors and my name" because "my cousin and my sister tellin' me I write my name chicken scratch. But I don't." (I asked Makisha for the definition of chicken scratch and she replied, "It means it's a chicken. It's like scribble scrabble.")

Makisha emphatically declares that while she knows that kindergarten will teach her new literacy skills, she doesn't entirely need this future experience for her literacy education. She already can write her name well, even though some family members don't think so. Makisha, as well as her peers, already have a strong sense and awareness of their developmental talents as defined by home and school. They also have a keen sense of how preschool and kindergarten fit into this larger scheme of child development and literacy learning at home and school. Makisha knows that she must answer to the expectations of school and also to the expectations of home and family in regard to literacy achievement and performance—and that the two must go hand in hand for her to be successful and admired in both places of experience, learning, and socialization. She senses, at a young age, that she must have a strong voice in her own efforts to meld development, diversity, and literacy. Makisha, like her peers, already has the knowledge that building successful bridges between development and diversity is founded upon getting bigger and getting smarter against the particular backdrops of school, family, friends, and community.

Part III

Widening Circles of Literacy

Lynn with daughters Nadyiah and Artisha, and son Alex

Aida with daughters Sonia and Areli

Chapter 6

Literacy and Schooling–
The Perspectives of Teachers

I love to read books. That's the first thing that you need to let the kids know. You need to show that enthusiasm to kids–if they don't see that, then they think, "Why should I care?"
                                                    –Robin, an early childhood teacher

I talked with preschool and elementary school teachers in the district about their views on developmentally appropriate and responsive literacy teaching. All of the preschool teachers worked at the preschool sites where I taught, and all of the kindergarten teachers had taught students from the district's preschools.

LITERACY AND CHILD AND FAMILY DIVERSITY

I spoke with Pandora and denise, two teachers who work closely together at my former elementary school. Pandora, an African American woman, is in her second year of teaching. denise, also an African American woman, is a veteran elementary school teacher and mother of two children. Both teach kindergarten and first grade, keeping their students for two consecutive years.

I asked Pandora and denise about what they hoped their incoming kindergarten children would have learned and experienced in preschool.

DENISE: In an ideal situation, children will come in [to kindergarten] with lots of language experiences—from stories to poems. Wherever parents are, traveling on a bus, they are *talking* to their kids. It's important for kids to know how to talk and how to be talked to; it's important for them to learn how to be involved in a language experience. I'd rather see that than children learning their ABCs.

PANDORA: It's important for children at this age to name their reality, to know their friends and to know how to have a conversation. It's important for them to describe what they like and what they want to do.

DENISE: I see children who have been forced to pen and paper, and are
not really ready for this. Some things I give them in kindergarten,
the kids will say, "We did this in preschool." They shouldn't have
been doing that in preschool. When children are working on things
that they are not ready for, incorrect ways of doing things become
fossilized, like handwriting, for example. When kids are forced to
do handwriting in preschool, versus sand and water and making
big motions, then their pen and paper work becomes fossilized and
it's hard to get them out of it. So I go *back* to *preschool* and do
scissors and glue and clay and tearing paper.

While not arguing against attention to literacy form in preschool, denise
and Pandora would rather have children enter kindergarten having experienced activities such as "scissors and glue and clay and tearing paper"
because they provide developmentally appropriate and meaningful learning experiences.

I asked Pandora, as a new teacher, if her teacher training had provided
experience and knowledge of the developmental capabilities of preschoolers.
She explained:

I had a roommate who was a preschool teacher and some family
and friends also taught preschool. But I had *no* preservice information on preschool. It could have helped. It would have given me a
concept of the first 2 months of kindergarten; if the kids *don't* meet
those expectations, should I then be concerned? If they don't write
their names by October, that it's possible that it will click later. In
general in my preservice training, I was not taught that it's real
repetition and process, and if children are given models and
chances for skills that you're trying to build with them, *then* it *will*
click for them. Now I'm teaching first grade. I see that—the process
and concept revisiting, and seeing things in different ways, it *will*
click.

When I asked how she developed her literacy teaching, she said:

As a new teacher, I started teaching and I felt that I didn't know
anything about the learning process. I had a lot of process and ideas
from my preservice training. denise helped me *not* be afraid to teach
phonics, and *not* to jump on the bandwagon of just surrounding
kids with books and assuming they will magically learn how to
read. This is *not* how I learned to read. So it's really teaching that
has worked, not reconstructing the wheel, but *adapting* it to the kids

of today. I just want to make sure that I'm using things that work and have worked for others.

Through the hands-on guidance of a more experienced teacher, Pandora has learned not to be "afraid to teach phonics" and not to jump "on the bandwagon of just surrounding kids with books and assuming they will magically learn how to read."

I asked Pandora her thoughts on successful literacy teaching for African American children.

> I'm torn between people who aren't African American and those who are teaching African American kids. Teachers need a very clear understanding of the child and the community's experiences, and the whole picture of *that* child and community. My frustration is that the reality of the African American child in education today is the absence of African American educators in their lives. Experience is the best teacher, and so someone with experiences that will relate to a child's experiences *may* be able to relate and collaborate with a child's growth and learning experiences. I feel that it is important for African American educators to come together and hash out what works and what doesn't for our kids in the educational system. What models can we take from our sister and brother cultures, and what models can we take from the world? There are teachers who are doing things that work. It's an all-out call, a state of emergency, and we need to come together.

Pandora cautions that teachers who teach African American children "need a very clear understanding of the child and the community's experiences, and the whole picture of *that* child and community." This does not mean that only African American teachers can teach African American children well (Ladson-Billings, 1994), but that teachers need a clear understanding of children's educational and cultural lives.

I asked denise about her views on effective literacy teaching for diverse learners. She told me:

> I teach from my passion, and so the community that I teach to is able to share in my story. I like to immerse children in a variety of language experiences: storytelling, story writing, acting out stories, and reading wordless books. The variety of language experiences allows children to wade in the water of words; they're reading their world! But I do feel that kids need to have practice. With the diversity in classrooms—cultural, skill level, experiences, and so

on—it is important to expose children to an array of learning opportunities. I appreciate a program that has a sound skills approach to it. I do not support the separation of a skill-based program versus whole language. Developmentally appropriate curriculum, whole language, and a skill-based program—they're all part of one big whole. Leaving the skills aspect out reduces the chances of a teacher reaching and teaching to the diversity of the classroom community.

As an experienced teacher, denise sees historically disparate literacy frameworks as really "part of one big whole," and particularly argues for the place of literacy skills in kindergarten and first grade.

When I asked denise for her views on the role of preschool in preparing diverse learners for this kind of elementary school teaching, she said:

> I expect preschool to be a lot of language experiences, and not a lot of formal skill-based stuff. Getting children to talk, to read their world, and validate their stories should be a *huge* part of preschool. Empowering children with oral language skills is a move into other skills they will learn later like reading. I have children in my [kindergarten] class who can sing the ABC song but have no idea what the letters are and what sounds they make. They are struggling in kindergarten! Take a child who enters kindergarten with some letter recognition and loads of language/story experiences, and I bet this child will do well in kindergarten. They have a strong literacy base to work from. Let the children talk in preschool and as they progress through kindergarten and first grade the attention to more detailed skills can come into play. Before formalizing their literacy skills, they need to live and talk about their stories!

Both Pandora and denise value the affirmation of children's cultural and personal identities through their personal stories *and* the teaching of particular literacy skills. It is through the combination of attention to children's lives and literacy conventions that children will thrive in their literacy learning.

LITERACY IN THE PRESCHOOL

I spoke with Jane and Gladys, who share a classroom of three-, four-, and five-year-olds at Casanova Preschool. Jane, an African American woman, has taught preschool for several years. Gladys, a Filipino American woman, also has taught preschool in the district for several years.

I asked Jane and Gladys about their general perspectives on preschool literacy education.

GLADYS: Jane and I have the same philosophy. We believe in the activities on the "practical life" [from Maria Montessori] shelf. We encourage the children to use scissors and practice cutting on the lines and on discontinued paint samples. Later on, they cut out catalogues.

JANE: They love to use ink markers and pens every day. They like to paint every day. Our indoor art area is open all the time. They love to "paint" the fence and the ground outside with water. We try to bring the art outside. We also use metal insets [Montessori material]. First, the children trace outside and then inside. They also love the clipboard. They write like they're in the office.

GLADYS: We also use sandpaper letters and they trace the letters with their fingers. Before we try to write their names, because they won't be ready, we emphasize their signing their work. It is also good for the children to be exposed to other fine-motor activities. Even if they can't write their names, they scribble their names. We also sing their names on the rug [during meeting time], have name tags, and we cover their photos [of their faces] and say, "If this is your name, you can wash your hands." We also sing Bingo and spell the child's name, A-S-H-A-Y-A-H.

JANE: And their names are all around the room, on their beds, birthday chart, counting pegs.

GLADYS: We label our whole room, from the computers to the doors to the materials.

JANE: And the kids call out the letters.

GLADYS: "What does this letter say?" they ask.

Gladys and Jane advocate attention to literacy forms in preschool, while also personalizing the children's experiences with alphabet- and letter-related activities. I asked Jane and Gladys for their views on the role of children's literature.

JANE: It's important for the children to learn how to turn pages in a book and in general to take care of the book. It's general knowledge of how to use the book.

GLADYS: Some of the children tear up the books. They have not had enough experience on how to handle books. They leave books on the floor and don't respect the books. So we tape the books up together when they're damaged. The children have improved;

we've incorporated a quiet reading time after lunch. The children
read on their mats or share a mat with a friend. They especially like
the books with the transparencies and photographs of live animals.
And the children love to pretend to be teachers when they read,
even if there's no audience!

JANE: They like to show the pictures as if they have an audience. They
mimic us by reading and then holding up the book for the imaginary audience to see the pictures. They especially do it now that
we're reading longer books like *Green Eggs and Ham*.

Jane and Gladys want to guide children in the "general knowledge" of how
to "respect" and take care of books, such as properly turning the pages and
returning books to their shelves.

JANE: Later in the year, after training them how to take care of the
books, the children want the books fixed.

GLADYS: After nap time, two children pick up books and put them
away. They take all the books and put them back on the shelves.
They even take the books that other kids hide under their [sleeping]
mats. The older kids are especially good at putting the books back
on the shelves.

I asked about the role of basic literacy skills in their literacy teaching.

GLADYS: We've been doing a lot of work with manipulative objects and
initial sounds. We use the small tubs of objects that all start with the
same letter. Our kids have been amazing. We also use a dry erase
board to draw pictures and then write the letters for the beginning
sounds of the animals or objects. The children say "t" and "tuh" for
"tiger." The other day I kept drawing and writing letters. We went
for half an hour since everybody wanted to say a word.

JANE: Whatever animal we draw and write, the children remember.
Most of the time, we only have to do it once, and the children
remember. Since our current theme is animals, this morning I drew
a dinosaur and we brainstormed other objects that also started with
"d." We also do a letter a week. We immerse the children in activities around that letter. First, we introduce the letter and the sound it
makes with the small tubs of manipulatives. We then learn vocabulary and write down all the words that start with that letter. We fill
the board up.

GLADYS: One child thought of "ukulele" the other day! Another child
thought of an unusual animal that she remembered from one of our

computer games. We then move our fingers along sandpaper letters and say the letter's sound.

JANE: We also use a computer game, which shows how to write the letter and says the letter's name. When you click on a picture of a child, he jumps for the letter "j." We also then make a letter book with the whole class.

GLADYS: Next, we decorate the letters. For "p," we use popcorn on pink paper. For "s," we use mosaic squares. For "t," we decorate triangles.

In this ordered approach to introducing children to letters and sounds, Jane and Gladys want the children to have "concrete experiences with objects to manipulate," and their approach "gives the children confidence" and gets everybody "involved."

I also spoke with Ruthie, an African American woman who teaches at Hawthorne, and who is a veteran early childhood teacher in the district. She explained:

One of the main things that I'd like to see is for children to leave preschool as achievers as opposed to being nonachievers. With adequate resources and teacher support, this *can* be possible. I do support reading; if you don't do anything else, read to your kids at home, read to your kids at school. With the bookbag program at Hawthorne, the kids are so interested. All the kids say, "Teacher Ruthie, I brought my bookbag today."

For Ruthie, as for Gladys and Jane, preschool helps children become "achievers," and literacy plays an important role in this process.

There are some basic skills children need to learn. We have the children's names on the cots. When the kids get on the wrong cot, we show them that this name begins with this letter. That's letter recognition, the first process. We'll introduce other parts, and the kids will put letters together and then words into sentences. This is a step into effective reading. I've seen it work with most children.

I asked Ruthie about her role in establishing a successful learning environment for her children.

I have become more of a facilitator. I set up centers and age-appropriate activities. This is an integrated curriculum as opposed to a more structured curriculum. Sometimes, if it's too structured, the behavior of kids changes. You want to help the kids to develop self-esteem and you want to have high expectations, and also to have the kids enjoy their learning as opposed to not wanting to come to school.

Ruthie also expressed the view that preschool is a place to get ready for kindergarten.

Kindergarten plays a big role. The expectations of kindergarten are high now. When kids get ready to leave preschool, the kindergarten teachers expect certain skills like an increased attention span and emotional skills. I believe in teaching some academic skills and I believe in readiness. Some children may *not* be ready to write their names, but if you expose kids and provide the materials, then kids get the opportunity. Not all kids grow at the same rate. Teachers need to observe kids and see if kids need to be introduced to numbers, letters, and writing their names. Some kids learn to write their names at home. With Charles—we didn't teach him his name—but only the ABCs with Bingo and tiles and the blackboard. He wrote his name. I was totally impressed. "Oh, you wrote your name!" So we introduce these things to the kids.

For Ruthie, preschool is a place to get ready for kindergarten, and a big part of this readiness involves basic literacy skills. Ruthie cautions, though, against teaching such skills to all children and advocates observing "kids to see if they need to be introduced to numbers, letters, and writing their names."

I also spoke with Robin, a male Asian American teacher, who has taught preschool and primary-grade children.

One of my strong points is reading books. I love to read books. That's the first thing that you need to let the kids know. You need to show that enthusiasm to kids—if they don't see that, then they think, "Why should I care?"

Robin believes in the power of a teacher's personal power and authority (Ladson-Billings, 1994) to reach children and encourage a love for literacy.

It's essential to bring excitement to the voice. When there's some-thing exciting in the book, change the intonation in your voice, show in your face that you're excited. Whisper the voice, yell the voice. Here's an example that I brought. It's *Dinosaur Roar!*

(Strickland & Strickland, 1994). I like to read books that are colorful and short. (opens to the first page) The book shows the children the concepts of strong and weak, high and low, big and small. I don't say, "Dinosaur roar." I say, "Dinosaur ROAR!!!" That stops the children right there. You can see right there that they can see it's going to be a fun book.

For Robin, the power of literacy for children lies in the performance (Dyson, 1993, 1997) of sound, sense, and the visual. As the central protagonist, Robin gives drama to books, as "dinosaur ROAR!!!" "stops the children right there."

This picture illustrates the fierceness of the dinosaur, and compares it to the small dinosaur. Then I hide my face *behind* [to hide from the dinosaur] the book to illustrate what the author is showing: This dinosaur is big and strong, "Don't mess with me!"

I asked Robin about the value of turning children's literature into performance for diverse learners. He explained:

For second-language learners, just by reading the book and reading the word, it speaks for itself. Then at the end of the book, I go back and say right here, "Do you know what this word 'meek' means?" Some will know, and I also explain it. "Dinosaur *fast*." I say it quickly and the kids laugh. "Dinosaur slooowwwwwww." And the kids are dying right now . . . sometimes they lose focus at this point. They yell out, "I can beat you!" "I can run fast." The children already know the concepts of fast and slow from running around outside—this reinforces it for them. (turning the next page) "Dinosaur above" and "dinosaur below." For "above," here I stand up and hover over my group. For "below," I get down low. (turning the next page) "Dinosaur weak" and "dinosaur strong." For "weak," I make my voice scraggly. For "strong," I flex my biceps. And you know what the kids are doing . . . they're flexing [their biceps]. "Dinosaur fat" and "dinosaur tiny." "Can you tell me what this is?" They'll all say "fat." I'll show them with my tummy sticking out. "Can you see the small dinosaur?" A lot of the three-year-olds don't know "tiny," but they know "small," so they say "small" or "little." I say, "There's another word for that," and I show it with my two fingers, like this.

Aware of important needs of children learning a new language, Robin provides language in small, manageable chunks and provides new vocabulary in context and through intonation and gestures (Tabors, 1997). For children who bring their diversity of ways of interacting with others around language into the classroom (Au & Jordan, 1981), Robin provides opportunities in a group literacy setting to call out ("I can beat you." "I can run fast") and to participate in socially inclusive ways ("For dinosaur strong, I flex my biceps. And you know what the kids are doing . . . they're flexing [their biceps])."

I asked Robin how he balances children's developmental capabilities with his literacy goals and strategies. He described:

> When the children get into the book, I feel that it makes the book more exciting and gets them involved. It's better than just sitting listening to the story read by the teacher. I allow the children a certain amount of time to say or show how they feel at the time— 10 or 20 seconds. I start making the transition between preschoolers and older elementary-age children. With older children, I don't allow as much involvement because older kids usually have better self-control. They're supposed to know how to sit still and focus versus three- and four-year-olds. They're still trying to learn how to do all that versus listening to a teacher ramble on in a monotone. Get the kids involved, get them excited.

Robin's sense of himself as a strong teaching personality propels the developmental and responsiveness aspects of his literacy practices and perspectives.

I also spoke with Connie, an African American woman who teaches at Casanova Preschool. An experienced early childhood educator, Connie also teaches child development classes at a district high school.

> I want my preschool children to have an awareness of print in preschool, and so I fill the environment with lots of print. I do a lot of stories, and sometimes do impromptu stories where I start a story and the children finish it. We also take dictation and write down what the kids say to make their own story books. In addition, I add in some letter recognition for children to know at least some of their sounds by the time they go to kindergarten. Although most preschoolers can't read, this lays a foundation for learning how to read later. Once they're clear on /ah/ for "A," they'll think of "A" for "Africa."

For Connie, as for the other preschool teachers, attention to literacy as meaningful print and as skill development for later reading are both important preschool literacy goals.

For writing, I use some Montessori materials like sandpaper, where the children trace the letter. Before actually writing, you *have* to do lots of activities to develop the hand, like scooping and pouring, and not just give kids paper and pencil. We also use the movable [Montessori] ABCs to form words, and the children build the words themselves. We also use three-part cards where children match pictures of a cat to each other, and also match the words "cat" to each other on another card.

For Connie, writing, like reading, is important in preschool, and it is valuable developmentally for children first to develop their fine-motor skills. I asked Connie whether she teaches in different ways to a mixed-age class, and she said:

At circle time, I always start with things that are good for both age groups of children: fingerplays, songs, rhymes, and lots of repetition. I start with a foundation for the younger children and then go on to what's developmentally appropriate for them. But there are some four-year-olds who can do something that five-year-olds can't do, so you have to be in touch with what *individual* children can do. You just can't go by chronological age.

Connie gave me her views about developmentally appropriate teaching in diverse classrooms.

Developmentally appropriate teaching is the ideal and the norm for that age group. But you then have to *break it down* to what's developmentally appropriate for *that* child. And that's the hard part because you have to fine-tune your teaching in a large class to each child.

Since breaking down language and tasks (Moore, 1998) is crucial in responsive teaching, Connie "breaks down" activities into what is appropriate for each individual child's needs.

I asked Connie about her role in starting children's educational careers in preschool.

In preschool, I want to be loving and warm and meet the children's basic needs. When they're older, I want to see them graduate and go to college. Preschool makes learning fun and allows them to explore and ask questions. So you always need to answer the children, and feed them spoonfuls of information as they are ready for them. They say you're not supposed to do a lot of worksheets in preschool, and they're correct if it's all just rote learning. But depending on your teaching style, you can teach anything by making it concrete and fun. The children are eager. You can see it in their eyes.

I asked Connie for her views on scribble scrabble.

It's part of the developmental process! They have to go through scribble scrabble. It doesn't turn me off, though there is a distinction between scribble scrabble when kids are doing it purposively and when kids are doing it developmentally. In the latter situation, it tells me that I need to work with that child to develop their fine-motor skills for learning to draw and write.

For Connie, "purposeful" scribble scrabble refers to children's scribbling when they are capable of doing something else. "Developmental" scribble scrabble refers to the place where children are in their drawing and writing, and their scribble scrabbling indicates to Connie where she can work with them.

FROM PRESCHOOL TO KINDERGARTEN

I spoke with both preschool and kindergarten teachers and one elementary school principal about the role of literacy in connecting preschool to kindergarten. Louise is an Anglo-Jewish woman who has taught preschool and currently teaches kindergarten and is a certified Reading Recovery teacher. I asked Louise about how the new California standards for kindergarten–grade 12 reading and writing have affected her literacy teaching.

The kindergarten standards have changed dramatically. If all children had excellent preschool programs, and literacy support from home, we could meet many of these standards. But many kids don't have the quality preschool experiences. There are, of course, a variety of preschool experiences that will work—lots of books, lots of stories, lots of books that the children will be familiar with in kindergarten. I don't expect preschools to be different from what they've always been: daily story time, lots of good books, a language arts time with finger plays and songs, listening station, the chance to listen to books over and over again, and teachers who love literacy and read as part of their daily life. Given these things, and home literacy support, most kids can meet the current state standards. If not, as a kindergarten teacher, I need to provide the richness of a preschool program *and* try to meet the specific standards of kindergarten.

For Louise, a kindergarten teacher with extensive early childhood experience, meeting all the state standards for all her students has proven problematic. She does not see preschool entirely as a place for basic skills in literacy, or as a place solely for fun and playing with materials. Rather, Louise argues for preschool as a social and educational experience that provides high-quality experiences with books and words and songs within a warm and vibrant human environment.

I asked Louise about developmentally appropriate practice, responsive teaching, and the literacy standards.

> The kindergarten standards don't take into account the diversity of preschool and family experiences that our kids have. The standards don't have built into them, in a meaningful way, a developmental understanding to meet kids' needs. I wouldn't want to see preschool standards developed. There should be standards of excellence for the preschool *program* but *not* standards of performance for the children. For me, it's important to ask if the standards being adopted are responsive to the needs of kids and families.

For Louise, the standards emphasize children's literacy performance rather than the overall quality of a school or literacy program. The standards, then, hold the literacy learning of all individual children against one single set of expectations. The new standards also require teachers to be more creative to meet the developmental needs of children and the specifics of the standards.

> It's important to make the curriculum responsive to the children. You don't want to take a child who comes in with little experience with the alphabet and expect the child to learn all 26 letters by the end of the year, without *also* expecting a rich language experience along the way of learning the 26 letters. We need kids' reading and writing to have rich symbolism and ideas. In other words, in teaching to the standards, we need also to teach rich language and ideas.

Louise sees the value of teaching to the standards, and of paying attention to discrete literacy forms as preparation for becoming readers and writers, while also emphasizing a responsive and meaningful curriculum.

For example, I'm making an alphabet chart of fruit and vegetables. We're eating apples, blueberries, coconuts, dates, endive, and figs. It's not only a question of developmentally appropriate practice; it's taking a task that could be sterile, and making it rich and creative. My kids now know that figs are imported from Greece, that you can buy them at a store, that they grow in Selena's [one of the children in the class] garden, and they start with the letter "f," which is the same as "fish" and "foot." So we've got a developmentally appropriate language arts project that takes less than 5 minutes a day. I provide something outside the normal classroom materials and link it to children's experiences.

For Louise, important elements of developmentally appropriate curriculum and responsive instruction can effectively come about in concentrated, imaginative bursts of literacy education. It comes about through helping her students "dig knowledge out" (Ladson-Billings, 1994) to uncover the deeper layers of literacy and learning.

I asked Louise about teachers' own developmental paths in reaching this level of teaching.

How to put it all together? This requires skill and the experience of being a responsive teacher. It is why you need teachers who are well trained and continually involved in staff development. I've been teaching for a long time and constantly learning new things to do. For example, nursery rhymes—why bother to teach them at all? They're so old-fashioned. Yes, but they are part of an intellectual history. They have rhyme and good vocabulary. "*Fetch* a pail of water." Are they sexist? Yes. You can change them. Take the base material and use it in a variety of ways. For kids to grow up now, and not experience nursery rhymes, means that they miss out on all sorts of other language experiences. So, I set as a goal for all of my kids to have a base in a couple of nursery rhymes which they can recite, paint about, sing about, and read *in context*. You can build this base in preschool. If kids don't have that base in preschool, you have to read these books more than once in kindergarten. And it's good to do it in small groups. They get the idea very quickly— sophisticated ideas about plot and character and rhyme—when kids work with a common knowledge base.

For Louise, connecting literacy development and diversity means constantly trying out new ideas and practices. It also means paying attention to certain literacy forms and functions while tailoring activities to meet children's individual needs and experiences.

I also spoke with Leilani, Louise's kindergarten colleague. Leilani, who is Filipina, is also a former preschool teacher and currently a certified Reading Recovery teacher. Leilani gave me her visions for children's preschool learning.

> I'd like them to have a wide array of experiences based on a balance of structured and open-ended activities. Open-ended activities allow preschoolers to express their individuality more readily. For example, activities involving play dough, book browsing, and dramatic arts promote the sharing of common experiences. Both kinds of activities take the kids from what they know to what I want them to know. It is important to have a variety of conversations and activities where they can share their experiences and build on them. A cooking project is a good example of incorporating the kids' personal experiences and introducing them to new concepts at the same time. I can ask, "How do you use this ingredient at home?" or "What does your family use instead?" "Where do you think the water goes when the rice is cooked?" "If we need three cups of rice and five cups of water, how many cups will we have in the pot?" This is the heart of preschool learning where kids learn through concrete experiences.

I asked Leilani for her thoughts on helping children get off to a successful start in kindergarten.

> This is largely dependent on the teacher. For many children, linguistic and behavioral expectations at school are different from what they are used to at home. For example, in my kindergarten circle time I have certain expectations for the children: They're expected to sit down, be still, take turns listening, and talk on-topic. But this is not all that I do. For some families, using oral language is not common practice and so this activity is difficult. And then there are those families where conversations overlap and "chiming in" is perfectly acceptable. So I modify all this so students feel they belong in the classroom. I allow call-and-response for kids who benefit from it, and for the quieter children I have a time when they turn to their neighbor and share their favorite part of a book. Children should *not* have to choose

between their home and school cultures—each should ideally complement each other. This is where the art of teaching comes in, and my role as teacher is critical.

Preschool, then, is an important early learning place for children to prepare for kindergarten, which Leilani sees as a continuation and not an entirely new starting point.

I asked Leilani for her expectations of children's literacy learning upon entering kindergarten.

> Knowing the alphabet and the sounds is a small part of the big picture. The big picture is introducing children to good stories, and having these stories enhance their lives. I'd rather see kids book browsing and listening to stories than see them copy letters that have no meaning for them. When they enter kindergarten, I want to see eager learners, children who are excited about books and sharing and telling their own stories. It makes me sad to see children come in knowing their ABCs, but already burnt-out at the beginning of kindergarten.

I asked Leilani about the influence of the new kindergarten language arts standards.

> It's easy for teachers to think of activities that are top-down in order to achieve the standards. In this kind of thinking, the kids are the last ones teachers may think of. They are not incorporating the kids' interests or developmental capabilities by building on what the kids *know*. What happens is that teachers tend to focus on what kids *don't* know, and the activities tend to be centered around their weaknesses instead of their strengths.

Leilani provided an example of a child she taught in kindergarten and currently is working with in Reading Recovery.

> For example, when I taught one particular child in kindergarten I was expected to bring her up to a certain reading level. I was also supposed to teach her the "mechanics" of reading like one-to-one correspondence and beginning letter sounds. One leveled book had a story about forest animals that included a hedgehog, and this child was pointing to the hedgehog, and didn't know what it was. So kids need field trips and other stories to give them some background information on what these stories are about, so they know

firsthand the difference between farm animals and wild animals. Kids need to see the animals and have a personal experience with what they're reading. You want to pique their curiosity, and part of this is going to motivate them to read. Otherwise, reading just becomes a pointing activity where teachers sit quietly and take running records. There's no conversation and no direct interaction with children, and reading becomes a task rather than something that brings joy and richness to their lives.

For Leilani, literacy skills in both preschool and kindergarten need to be grounded in experiences of the world that make good developmental and responsive sense to children. Otherwise, children receive a surface experience with literacy where teachers take on a distant role ("reading just becomes a pointing activity where teachers sit quietly") and books are disconnected from the real world ("Kids need to see the animals and have a personal experience with what they're reading").

I also spoke with Becky, the district's former Director of Child Development and current principal of Casanova Elementary School, who said:

I think we really need to do more literacy in preschool. As we know more and more about how students learn to read, it's critical for preschools and elementary schools to promote best practices in literacy. We're involved in CELL [California Early Literacy Learning] right now. It's a program that focuses on best practices in literacy: shared and guided reading, interactive writing, and some others. It's a 3-year commitment and we have one teacher from four grade levels [Connie, from Casanova Preschool, and one teacher each from Casanova's kindergarten through grade three classrooms] working together as a team. We in education need to figure out more connections with the preschools. Programs like CELL do help kids do well in literacy. Early childhood is such a critical time for literacy education and development.

For Becky, best practices with literacy education provide ongoing staff development, and a team approach (such as CELL) links preschool with elementary school teachers. Becky argues, too, as does the State of California (*Continuity for Young Children*, 1997; *Every Child a Reader*, 1995), for the importance of quality literacy experiences as a foundation for kindergarten.

A literacy emphasis in preschool can really help children. There is such an immense range in our kindergartens. Some children enter kindergarten not knowing how to handle a book. It is helpful in learning how to read to know the concept of going across the page, and then sweeping back, and other aspects of book handling and reading. Other children enter kindergarten with a sense of what to do: They know about the book's title, author, know to start "reading" at the top of the page, and they have a wealth of experience with phonemic awareness. So we need to do more in preschool. Definitely you can teach children to read in elementary school using best practices such as CELL and Reading Recovery. But it's an uphill battle in the early elementary years. We're putting more resources into the K–3 strand; if the kids don't read by grade three, their chances are pretty slim of reading well.

For Becky, preschools are an important place for exposing and introducing children to various aspects of literacy education that provide a foundation for kindergarten literacy competence.

I asked Becky about possible bridges between developmentally appropriate and responsive literacy education.

It can be both. Having activity centers and play—it can be a balance. I'd never say to teachers, "Don't have the blocks and the dollhouse. But I wouldn't give kids the chance not to come to story time." The teachers' responsibility is to make story time so interesting and varied that everyone wants to come. And teachers can cover basics here—the cover of a book, this is how you open a book—and also more sophisticated language—making predictions and talking about character. We can't rely on the children constructing this all on their own. This is the time when the teacher has to take the lead; children really need to come to story time and participate. I'm trying to say this is the way of expansive literacy: *not* just the letter "A" and the letter "B," but reading the stories, rhyming, hearing and playing with the sounds are an important part of a very rich program.

I asked about her vision for an "expansive literacy" within the preschool to kindergarten transition.

I think that we have to do it *really* well. In the ideal world, we need to work closely together as elementary and preschool educators. Sometimes for preschool teachers, the range for literacy education is like this [moves her hands close together], when it really needs to be like this [moves hands wider apart]. The value of CELL and other best practices lies in their long-term implementation and in the preschool–elementary school teamwork.

I asked Becky for her thoughts on how teachers judge their own teaching effectiveness in light of the new California literacy standards.

> What the State [of California] does, affects our teaching. There is not much meeting in the middle. The state standards are coming from the top, and changes in schools are coming from the bottom. There is no middle ground, and the benchmark is standardized testing. This is not working on the curriculum from the bottom up. I think that some of the standards for kindergarten and grade one are not developmentally appropriate. We have now moved from the concept of kindergarten getting children ready to read to first grade, where we teach reading. When we teach reading, and when you read the grade one standards, many of our students are not there. The best we can do is to use programs that use best practices. For a number of teachers, those who are brand-new and those on emergency credentials, the bar on the standards is too high. No teacher wants to fail and feel frustrated. It's a simplistic statement to say that if you only have high expectations, then you'll teach well. It's much more complicated than that. I think we're in quite a dilemma: when the standards are for children with a high level of literacy—and maybe they are meeting them—but to take a child with only beginning phonemic awareness from preschool and say to a teacher, "This is the standard and you have to have high expectations, and obviously you haven't done a good job by the end of the year." This can be really demoralizing to teachers.

Responsible for the developmental learning of her teachers, and especially beginning teachers, Becky argues for a reconceptualization of the literacy standards so teachers can feel successful early in their teaching careers.

THE ROLE OF PARENTS

I spoke with the preschool and kindergarten teachers about the role of parents in literacy education and about successful strategies for strengthening the home–school connection. One teacher, denise, said:

> As an elementary school teacher, I value the parent as the child's first teacher, and I let my parents know this! I try from the beginning to build a bridge between home and school. With the public preschools, the relationship is not always as strong. Public, state-run preschools require parents to either be full-time students or work full-time. Most families in these preschools do not hold

professional jobs and many live in subsidized housing. It is a different community and so the outreach to the community has to differ. Since many families in public preschools have not had good or connected relationships with schools, it is vital to make every effort to pull these families in.

An advocate for parent outreach, denise would like to see more parents involved in preschools and gain positive experiences in working in schools.

I also asked denise for her thoughts on changing current structures for preschool parent participation.

> There should be a home–school liaison that can call and make home visits to get these parents involved. Alter government regulations and maybe instead of going to school full-time, parents could go part-time and spend the other part-time in their child's preschool. Also, begin to run the government preschools more like the private cooperatives. This is transformative education at the preschool level! This empowers parents and builds a strong relationship between home and school and validates the parent's place as the first teacher! When I was a parent at a private cooperative preschool, I knew what my kids were doing. It was a partnership and the home–school connection was set.

Valuing the active role of parents, denise emphasizes the importance for preschools to help parents develop preset expectations of themselves as advocates for their children and see teachers as partners.

I also asked Ruthie about the role of parents in the preschool.

> As a preschool teacher, I think there should be a lot of parental involvement. It's very very important. You need the cooperation of the parents and for them to support their teacher. Parents have different skills and can be an asset to our program like when the parents took over the bookbag program for a while.

Given her years of teaching experience, I asked Ruthie about today's parents and their relationship to their children's schools.

> Parents are younger now, very young. There are young grandparents, too. Yes, parents do need to have help from teachers to have an effective and valuable experience as parents of preschoolers. That's what it's all about. It's important for the children that this

> kind of experience follows them into their adult years so when they
> look back, they can remember that they had a positive preschool
> experience. I always see my old students and they still remember
> me. They say, "This is my old preschool teacher!"

Ruthie connects the value of parental involvement with the success of
their children, and further links early school experiences with life-long
learning.

I asked Robin about general ways for teachers to strengthen connections with parents.

> My philosophy is not just about the kids. I like to work with the
> family. If it's not working at home, it's difficult to work at school.
> Parents have needs as well. If I can find out what's going on at
> home, it helps me relate to the kids at school. If I see that parents
> have no time to really be with their kids, I try to set up a conference
> to talk. I let them know that we need to work together to help the
> kids improve. Sometimes parents do make some changes, and, if
> not, I refer them to someone else who can help them.

For Robin, parents are central partners in their children's education, and
he works to create "a community of learners" (Ladson-Billings, 1994) by
involving parents.

I asked Robin about how he sees the literacy perspectives of his
parents.

> I think that parents who I know or I perceive to know to have some
> education, they determine what they want their kids to know. The
> higher the parents' education, the more they want their kids to
> know, and they'll *tell* me that. Other parents tell me that they want
> their kids to learn how to read, and how to write, and they tell me
> this in a general way. There are some other parents in the middle
> who may say, "I want my kid to do some phonics. You know, I
> want them to learn phonics and to read books." And they start off
> by saying, "You know." They don't say "sight words" or "compre-
> hension" like some other parents.

Robin believes in learning about the needs and expectations of parents, and
realizing that parents have varied literacy perspectives for their children.
Teachers in diverse classrooms, then, need to see the diversity of parental
perspectives on literacy education and the varied ways that parents may
express these views.

Pandora, a beginning teacher, improved her literacy teaching when denise "sat me down and showed me how to reflect on how things are done and *not* to be afraid to teach phonics, and *not* to jump on the bandwagon of just surrounding kids with books and assuming they will magically learn how to read."

denise, a veteran teacher, likes to "immerse children in a variety of language experiences: storytelling, story writing, acting out stories, and reading wordless books," which "allow children to wade in the water of words."

For Jane and Gladys, it is important for their preschoolers to "learn how to turn pages in a book and in general to take care of the book. It's general knowledge of how to use the book."

For Ruthie, it is important that her children "leave preschool as achievers as opposed to being nonachievers," and to "support reading; if you don't do anything else, read to your kids at home, read to your kids at school."

For Robin, literacy is an engaging dramatic performance, and it is important "to bring excitement to the voice. . . . Whisper the voice, yell the voice" when reading with children.

For Louise, "kindergarten [literacy] standards don't take into account the diversity of preschool and family experiences" and they "don't have built into them, in a meaningful way, a developmental understanding to meet kids' needs."

Leilani believes in the importance of children "not having to choose between their home and school cultures" because "each should ideally complement each other" through "the art of teaching and the critical role" of the teacher.

For Becky, "we in education need to figure out more connections with the preschools" because "early childhood is such a critical time for literacy education and development."

Learning to teach literacy from a colleague, helping children take care of books, building self-esteem through reading, linking literature and drama, meeting state standards, linking home and school, and connecting preschool with kindergarten: These are critical elements for improving and strengthening literacy education in preschool and elementary school as articulated by the early childhood educators.

Putting their perspectives and ideas into action is a challenge for those interested in literacy education in urban early childhood settings. For the teachers, it is really the moment-to-moment cooperation and dialogue that widen the circles of literacy for children and families. The teachers' perspectives on literacy evolve and change through a greater understanding of children's needs and capabilities as seen in daily teaching experiences in classrooms. It is hard, then, to look ahead and develop programs and visions for literacy education when much of this knowledge comes about slowly, on a day-to-day basis. But teachers (and children) can't wait, and so literacy education becomes a daily challenge of connecting appropriate and responsive literacy practices in preschool and elementary school, and watching and listening for the reactions of the children.

Chapter 7

Parents and Families–New Voices in Literacy Education

Writing letters and tracing *shouldn't* be mandatory [in preschool] because they're going to learn it in kindergarten anyway. Some things they should learn, but if they learn everything they'll be bored [in kindergarten]. So make it in the middle, a medium, if kids know how to write their names, they can write it over and over and over again.

–Rochelle, a parent of three children

Parents and families play crucial roles in expanding the circles of literacy for children and adults in schools. Given the critical relationship between literacy and parental empowerment in schooling (Ada, 1988; Delgado-Gaitan, 1996; Gadsden, 1994; Taylor, 1997; Valdés, 1996), and the need to broaden and diversify expectations of appropriate parental involvement and school literacy, we need to learn more about parental perspectives on literacy education.

THE BOOKBAG PROGRAM

At Hawthorne, I helped the teachers organize a home–school reading program. The school already had a large collection of canvas bookbags and a sizable collection of children's books. Over the course of 4 years, the teachers and I worked to build and improve the bookbag reading program. In the first year of the project, 67 parents signed up their children (out of a total of 91 children) for the program. In the second and third years, 61 out of 90 children enrolled. In the fourth year, 82 out of 90 children enrolled, and almost 50% of these children were actively reading their books on a weekly basis.

The program was designed to add a home–school component to the children's literacy involvement and to broaden their literary interests and experiences. The program's structure was designed to be manageable and flexible for the teaching staff. The children checked out a book of their choice from the Hawthorne library once a week and read the book at home with their parents, relatives, or older siblings. Once children had read 10 books, they received a small reading prize and a paper medal stating "You're a star reader!"

As a new project that involved a new kind of home–school connection and professional negotiation for the teachers, the program initially produced some tension among the staff and the parents. This tension decreased over time because the children became excited about checking out their own books, the teachers and I fine-tuned the check-out system and maintenance of the library, and the parents learned the program procedures and witnessed their children's enthusiasm. The higher number of children who enrolled by the fourth year of the project indicate the time and patience needed to develop a school-wide home–school literacy project. Nurturing a new layer of literacy that comfortably fits the particular social and literacy expectations and needs of the school community is not done easily or quickly.

In order to learn about the value of the program for parents, I spoke with Bonita, an African American woman who works as a teaching assistant in a nearby public school district. Bonita's daughter, Akilah, is currently a first grader who previously attended Hawthorne Preschool for 2 years. Bonita also has an older child in junior high school.

> I'm trying to think back on what skills Akilah learned when she left preschool, and what she knew how to do before she got to kindergarten. And I'm really thinking, I know this doesn't really count, but she had a respect for books. I don't know if this had anything really to do with the school, but I really do think that it did with the bookbag program that you guys had. She knew how to handle books, she knew how the book was organized from front to back, and she tried to recognize words like the easy "a"s and the "i"s. She tried to recognize the simple one-letter words. Her favorite words to try to figure out were "he" and "she." I don't know why, but she loved the words "he" and "she." So she tried to find those in the books she brought home.

For Bonita, the bookbag program provided Akilah with a home–school extension for learning about the world of books and for exploring their basic forms and functions. The project also gave Bonita concrete home experiences in reading with Akilah and watching and listening to Akilah's efforts to find such words as "he" and "she" in books.

> I like the check-out system for the bookbag program. I *really* enjoyed that. It gave the kids a sense of independence, and Akilah felt proud

to have her own book come home. She took care of it, and she wanted to read it as soon as she got home. She wanted to read *her* book. She knew that she had to take it back and she got to get *another* book. You know it's that whole independence factor, I guess. She really felt that was the special thing; if we left the house without *that* bookbag, she had a trauma. So we'd have to come back and get it. I think it was that something belonged to her. She also enjoyed going into the room and having the opportunity to choose and then to be read stories to. Whoever helped her, helped her pick some really good books. She brought a lot of African American books home and that was good because I probably wouldn't have just picked them up. You go to the kids' section at the library and you just don't pick up any book.

For Bonita, the bookbag program helped Akilah with the "whole independence" process, and provided the excitement that the "special thing" of the bookbag brought ("if we left the house without *that* bookbag, she had a trauma"). Bonita also liked that the program promoted a variety of books to read at home, and in particular introduced more "African American" books that Bonita "probably wouldn't have just picked up" on her own.

I asked Bonita for suggestions to improve the bookbag program.

It'd be good for the children to dictate something about their book. In kindergarten, Akilah did book reports and she dictated something about her book. It gives kids the opportunity to talk about their own book every now and then. It'd also be good to have something [like the book report sheet] to go home for parents to have a better idea of what to do in kindergarten. It'd also be good to have more parent meetings to teach about books; you can add a comment sheet with suggestions from parents. I think that some parents don't participate [in the Hawthorne bookbag program]— some have respect for books, and some don't have the time or don't care. If you have a book report, have it so kids can also do books at their house. It'd also be good to have a homework center at school.

Having seen Akilah go through kindergarten, Bonita sees the value of the preschool bookbag program in helping to prepare children for kindergarten literacy ("In kindergarten, Akilah did book reports and she dictated something about her book").

FAMILY LITERACY WORKSHOPS

I conducted family literacy workshops for parents at all the district's preschools and co-presented several sessions with preschool and kindergarten colleagues from the district. Partial support for the workshops was provided by small grants from a local educational funding source.

The primary goals of the workshops were to increase dialogue about literacy among families, introduce ways of reading with and to preschool-age children, introduce a variety of high-quality multicultural children's literature, and discuss children's literacy development and cultural and linguistic diversity. The workshops were attended primarily by the children's mothers, although a small percentage of fathers and grandparents also attended. At three of the preschools, Spanish translation was provided, and no-cost child care was provided at all sites for the preschoolers and their siblings.

By the fourth year of the workshop presentations, I crystallized a basic format: introductions by presenters and families, overview of workshop goals and purposes, description of various children's books, demonstration of strategies for reading with children, description of literacy extensions like art and science, a question and answer period, and an overview of a handout on reading strategies and lists of children's books. When the workshop ended, the children returned from child care to share in refreshments of juice and cookies and to select one free children's literature book to take home. Over refreshments, parents often asked the presenters individual additional questions for more information.

At the beginning of a session, I asked parents to tell their names and the names and ages of their children. This helped me adapt elements of the workshop toward books and strategies suitable for different age children. It also gave the parents an immediate chance to let their voices be heard and to know who the other parents were. I then sometimes asked the parents for questions about reading and writing with their children. I wrote these questions down on a large piece of paper, and either discussed them at the moment or returned to them later in the session. In these instances, parents contributed questions and issues ranging from wanting to know how often to read with their child to the appropriate content of books to read. The parents occasionally asked questions about older siblings who were in elementary school, and other questions involving kindergarten enrollment and access to bilingual education in the elementary schools. In addition, I varied the beginning of the workshop by asking parents to share something that worked for them in terms of literacy at home. In these instances, parents shared such ideas as making book reading "like homework" and "visiting the library every Saturday."

I also varied the middle sections of the workshop format. When I presented with colleagues, we each concentrated on a particular topic. For instance, in one workshop I discussed a small variety of different genres of books (fiction, nonfiction, wordless, rhymed, flap); Leilani, a kindergarten teacher, read one book to demonstrate enjoyable and effective ways to read out loud; and Louise, another kindergarten teacher, shared books by Ezra Jack Keats to demonstrate the value of getting to know books by one author.

PARENTAL PERSPECTIVES

I spoke with Bonita and several other parents to find out their perspectives and expectations for literacy education. In doing so, I hoped to uncover more information from the point of view of parents on finding common ground between developmentally appropriate and responsive literacy teaching.

In addition to Bonita, Akilah's mother, I highlight the perspectives of five other parents. Alma, a Hispanic woman born and raised in Mexico City, has three children who attended the Nieva and Bernard preschools. Her youngest daughter, Mariella, is currently in kindergarten, and her two older children, Ivan and Maria, are in second and third grade. All three children attend the same Spanish/English bilingual elementary school in the district. Alma currently works as a teaching assistant at the Nieva Bilingual Parent Nursery.

Rochelle is an African American woman with three daughters. Rochelle's youngest daughter, Jordanae, attends Hawthorne. Her older daughters, Jennifer and Jasmine, are in first and fourth grade. Rochelle teaches at a private, Christian preschool near Hawthorne. I spoke with Rochelle during the middle of Jordanae's last year at Hawthorne.

Regina is an African American woman studying for her A.A. degree in nursing. Her son Ryen is a three-year-old at Dorsey Preschool, and her daughters Brianna and Chatani are in fifth and eighth grade. I taught Brianna when she was in kindergarten and Chatani when she was in first grade. Brianna attended Hawthorne as a preschooler.

Lynn is an African American woman studying to become a computer repair technician. Her son Alex is a five-year-old in his last year at Hawthorne Preschool, and Lynn would like Alex to attend a Spanish immersion program for kindergarten. Lynn also has a 15–month-old daughter and a daughter in the eighth grade, Artisha, whom I also taught when she was in first grade.

Aida is a Latina woman who speaks Spanish and English. Aida has two daughters. Sonia is four years old and is in her second and last year at Hawthorne Preschool. Areli is ten years old and in fifth grade. Both Sonia and Areli speak Spanish and English.

Literacy and Schooling

The parents spoke with grace and sensitivity about what they wanted for their children's literacy education. Since some of the parents' children had left preschool or their preschool-age children had older siblings, the parents were also able to offer a long view of literacy education in preschool and beyond. This breadth of experience and knowledge about literacy enabled them to reflect on their own developmental journeys as parents and advocates for their children's education.

I asked Alma about her literacy goals for her children when they were in preschool.

> In my own experience, when kids come to kindergarten, they don't know what school is for. It makes for a hard situation for teachers and for parents. So in preschool, I wanted my children to know how to deal with it. I wanted them to learn their colors, shapes, count from one to 10, and identify the numbers. Most important, I wanted them to develop their attention, and be capable of listening for at least 10 minutes. What I also really wanted [in preschool] was playtime. I really liked the outdoor activities and I was concerned about a safe environment. I didn't care what program or subject of the month it was. I really respected the decisions of the teacher.

The specifics of a preschool literacy program do not interest Alma, although she is interested in her children having learned some basic numeracy and literacy skills. Alma also respects the role of the teacher and trusts the teacher's decisions and the program as educationally sound and beneficial for her children's overall growth.

> I've been going to the preschool here and I heard one parent saying, "What's the curriculum and the program for the year?" I think that in preschool this doesn't really matter. I don't think a three- and four-year-old cares about it. I really want the kids to really enjoy what they were doing—whatever the teacher was doing that day, whatever the subject, I was really grateful.

For Alma, her children's enjoyment of school is paramount; the specifics of curriculum and program of study are incidental in comparison with her children's overall developmental growth as children and as individuals. In arguing against a set curriculum, Alma refers to a developmental perspective of the interests and needs of children: "I don't think a three- and four-year-old cares about it."

I asked Alma if she worked on literacy skills and read books with her children at home.

> I never forced them to write their names. I was very interested in their fine-motor development. Sometimes you see kids who want to hold their pen, and they can't do anything with it. I didn't want them to write their names, but to practice drawing. (here Alma makes a sweeping back and forth gesture with her hand) I asked them what this [drawing] was, and they said, "A bird!" I was really happy that they were trying to draw what they wanted.

Although not interested solely in her children learning to write their names in preschool, Alma highlights the development of her children's fine-motor skills and their interests in drawing "what they wanted."

> I didn't encourage my kids to memorize books. I bought a big book by Alma Flor Ada, and I read it to them. I pointed to the left–right and the up–down directions for reading so they will know; and they do the same thing after me, and pretend with me. They started writing in uppercase in kindergarten and then they learned lower-case later. But in preschool I really wanted them to have a sense of touching water and of playing with the sand and going to the play dough area because I was interested in their fine-motor skills.

For Alma, having her children learn such basic aspects of book reading as the direction of reading print ("I pointed to the left–right and the up–down so they will know") is an important home literacy lesson. And yet Alma also values the role of play ("I really wanted them to have a sense of playing with the sand").

I asked Alma how she herself has developed as an educator of her children. She explained:

> Sometimes you don't know all the materials, and sometimes you want to reinforce what the teacher does. Sometimes you read stories to your kids the very traditional way, and it's not because you're old-fashioned. But you don't know the newer ways of teaching

kids. I've seen this book, *The Very Hungry Caterpillar*, and you put food in a big caterpillar puppet. I think that was great. And books on audio. Kids love that. I never knew they were available.

As a parent, Alma knows that she "reads stories to her kids the very traditional way, and it's not because you're old-fashioned. But you don't know the newer ways" and so she is open to learning them.

I talked with Bonita about her perspectives on preschool literacy for her daughter Akilah.

> I was thinking about her fine-motor skills when Akilah was in preschool, 'cause I know that's something important. I have an old book, an old preschool book that I had for my classes. So I went through it to see if I was being too sensitive or not sensitive about where she was at on her reading and writing. Like did I think that she should be able to read. Was I realistic? Was she supposed to be able to read? In order not to be stressed out, like saying to Akilah, "How come you can't read that?" I went back and did some research. And the book was saying that as long as she can sit for a period of time and the whole length of a book and actually understand what was said to her, this is the start of understanding reading. And she could do that. She understood what stories were. Akilah was able to sit there and that helped me to kind of not really stress out so much that she wasn't on track.

By doing "research," Bonita learned to see Akilah's literacy experiences in the larger context of her developmental capabilities ("as long as she could sit for the length of the story and understand the story"), which helped Bonita "not really stress out so much that Akilah wasn't on track" in her literacy learning.

When I asked Bonita if there were certain basic literacy skills she wanted Akilah to learn, she replied:

> Akilah got the recognition of her name, but I would have liked for her to have known how to write her first and last name, and not all in caps [capital letters] all over the paper. Also, for Akilah to understand the difference between upper- and lowercase. With a lot of help, I think she could have done it. Because if you start teaching them how to do it, the difference between the upper- and lowercase, they'll know. I just wanted something that she could do. She's so used to seeing them in uppercase that she didn't know that that was the same thing. If she saw a letter or word, and the first letter was

uppercase and the rest of the word was lowercase, she didn't realize that they were the same word as something all in caps. To her, it was something totally different. I actually did one of those things with her where one word was all uppercase and another all lowercase, and Akilah just didn't have an idea that they were the same thing. Kind of threw me off a little bit there! I just let it go. I told myself don't make a thing out of it. Don't stress. I'm learning to back off because I pushed and challenged Akilah's older brother, and I'm worried that those aren't the right tactics. And if it's going to happen in her learning, it's going to happen.

Although Bonita wants Akilah to have learned specific literacy skills in preschool, like distinguishing between uppercase and lowercase letters, Bonita has learned the value of "learning to back off because . . . if it's going to happen in her learning, it's going to happen" at some developmental point.

I asked Bonita if there were things Akilah does to promote her own literacy learning.

In kindergarten, she'd [Akilah] come home, pick up a phonics book—she was working on it at home—and she give herself some homework like her older brother. Akilah gets a phonics book and gives herself certain sections. She gets her own books and disciplines herself because I don't have to have that battle [that she had with her son]. I also give her a lot of positive reinforcement; a treat, that helped. Akilah is taking steps on her own, reading along with tapes, and it's just a matter of timing.

As a parent, Bonita is learning to adjust and change her ways of promoting Akilah's literacy growth. Having learned to give over a larger measure of control to Akilah, Bonita is glad "not to have that battle" that pits parent against child in working on school literacy.

I spoke with Rochelle, whose daughter Jordanae attends Hawthorne and whose older daughters attend first and fourth grade, about whether her views on preschool literacy education have changed over the years. She explained:

I saw preschool the same for each kid. Jasmine [the current fourth grader] had a different preschool [than Hawthorne]. They did things differently; it was a little more advanced. They had her learning simple words like "dog" and "cat." She knew her alphabets and all her numbers to 100. The teachers tried to keep her interested. She learned the ABCs from me and counting at school. She just looked at the numbers on the 1–100 chart in the classroom and loved it. The teachers didn't even know it. She learned on her own. She likes to explore and figure things out for herself. Sometimes now in fourth grade, she tends to still try to figure it out on her own instead of asking the teacher. All of my kids learn differently. With Jennifer, she's more outspoken. She's always raising her hand to ask questions [in school]. Jennifer did pretty good in preschool. She learned the basic stuff, her ABCs.

For Rochelle, it is important to recognize that her children approach school literacy in their own individual ways because "all of my kids learn differently."

I asked Rochelle if she had particular goals for her children's preschool literacy education.

I wanted all my kids to learn all the alphabet, at least the uppercase and also the lowercase would be helpful. In kindergarten, they learn how to write their name properly. So at least they can recognize the letters of their name [in preschool]; they can help kids with word and letter association, and help them know the letters. Writing their name in preschool is a little bit hard for everybody. I also wanted them to know their basic colors and shapes, stuff like that. Some things are basic; colors are everywhere, not just in school. Stop signs, clothes, they may not know what the stop sign says, but they know what it looks like.

Like Bonita, and to a lesser extent like Alma, Rochelle wants her children to "know their basic colors and shapes," to "learn all the alphabet," and "at least the uppercase" letters. Moreover, learning to recognize "lowercase" letters "would be helpful." Rochelle, though, recognizes that "writing their name in preschool is a little bit hard for everybody." She also values children's inclination toward the functions of print—her children "may not know what the stop sign says, but they know what it looks like."

Doing writing letters and tracing *shouldn't* be mandatory [in preschool] because they're going to learn it in kindergarten anyway. Some things they should learn, but if they learn everything they'll be bored [in kindergarten]. So make it in the middle, a medium, if kids know how to write their names, they can write it over and over and over again. For those who don't, they can learn it. For math, knowing the basic numbers is good enough. I don't think they need to add. Some preschools do. Sometimes if you're too advanced, the

kids get burned out, and the kids regress [later in kindergarten].
The kids have a whole life to learn, and they shouldn't be
pressured.

Rochelle sees a middle ground—"make it in the middle, a medium"—between her wishes for her children's literacy and her knowledge as a parent
and teacher about their developmental capabilities. To avoid school burn-
out (Elkind, 1981), Rochelle also argues that children "have a whole life to
learn, and they shouldn't be pressured" to achieve too many things too early.

When I asked Rochelle about her goals for her children's preschool
literacy education, she linked it to literacy learning in kindergarten.

It [learning some letters, shapes, colors in preschool] sets up a
foundation for kindergarten so kids don't go into it blindly. Even if
they repeat the same stuff in kindergarten, they'll have a better
knowledge of it. The basics will help. Preschool is also good for kids
to be with each other socially and to learn how to share, how to get
along with each other, work in small groups, as well as working
independently. The foundation starts in preschool, so when they get
in kindergarten, they'll already know it.

Aida, whose four-year-old daughter Sonia attends Hawthorne, also
wanted her daughter to be prepared for kindergarten. I asked Aida, as
Sonia and her older daughter Areli joined us for the interview, if there were
any literacy skills she wanted Sonia to learn by the end of preschool.

AIDA: Sonia already knows from home how to spell her ABCs. I taught
her. I asked her, "Sonia, write down an 'S' and an 'A' and an 'N.'"
By now she's OK with the letters. And she can also write her
numbers. She can write her telephone number. (Aida hands Sonia a
pen so she can write the numbers for me) She learned because I
taught her. She reverses some numbers, but if you ask her the
numbers, Sonia can tell you. I would also like her to recognize all
the numbers, and she can count to 100. Sometimes she gets stuck on
some numbers, and so I remind her and she keeps going.
ARELI: She also writes words and other numbers. My mom wrote the
words and numbers and Sonia copied them.
AIDA: She's a good copy. I also have these big cards with shapes and
objects on them. Sonia tells me what they are. She knows all the
colors and all the shapes. Sometimes when I am driving, she knows
when I need to stop from the stop sign and when I need to go when
it's green.

Aida, like the other parents, devotes time at home to learning basic literacy and numeracy skills. Like Rochelle, she sees how skills transfer to other activities ("sometimes when I am driving, she knows when I need to stop from the stop sign").

Aida and her older daughter Areli work together to promote Sonia's literacy learning both in and out of school.

ARELI: Sometimes I read out of a chapter book or a picture book, and after I read, we ask Sonia what happened. She does good. I learned from my mom because she did this with me. I also learned from my class at school because of book reports.

AIDA: And if I read a book today, and ask Sonia tomorrow or the next day, sometimes she remembers what the book was about.

ARELI: Also at [Sonia's] school, when the teacher reads a story, one that Sonia memorizes, she recognizes the books at home and in her class.

AIDA: At home, Sonia puts all her stuffed animals on the floor and reads to them with the book from the bookbag program. She likes to be the teacher. Sometimes she asks us to read the story.

ARELI: She also likes to copy the pictures [from the books] that she likes.

Areli, Sonia's sister, responds in her own developmental and responsive way to her sister's literacy needs and capabilities ("I read out of a chapter book or a picture book, and after I read, we ask Sonia what happened. She does good").

I asked Regina, whose daughters Chatani and Brianna joined us for the interview, about her goals and expectations for Ryen's (a three-year-old at Dorsey) literacy education at home and school.

I want Ryen to learn to recognize letters and numbers to a certain point. After he leaves preschool, though, and he's been there since 2.9 [years of age], he'll probably know the whole ABCs. He'll recognize the letters, the names of the letters, and a few sounds. I want him to at least recognize the names, that's the minimum. At home, we have the early readers and books with upper- and lowercase, and we just go through them and look at each page. Then when we go down the streets, Ryen says, "Oh 'P' and 'R.'" He especially says it for the letters in his name.

For Regina, learning tangible and concrete literacy skills is an important literacy goal in preschool. It is important to learn to recognize letters and numbers "up to a point," and to at least recognize the names of letters because "that's the minimum."

BRIANNA: When I ask Ryen how he spells his name, he'll say "R-Y-E-N."
     He smiles and he'll want me to draw a picture for him. He wants to
     write letters, so I write them down and he tries to copy.
REGINA: I try to take him to the library. I don't go often—not as much as
     I like with my schedule. In terms of books, Ryen loves to be read to.
     He memorizes. He can't read it, but he knows what it says.
BRIANNA: He reads to me. If he knows it himself, he says it. If he
     doesn't, I tell him.
CHATANI: I point at the pictures and read to him. If I say, what's in the
     picture? He tells me.
BRIANNA: He's got a good imagination.

As a family, Regina and her daughters influence and contribute to Ryen's
literacy learning. Brianna and Chatani know what delights their little
brother and where Ryen is and wants to go in his learning.

     When I spoke with Lynn, whose four-year-old son Alex attends
Hawthorne, we were joined by Artisha, her 14-year-old daughter. I asked
Lynn about her literacy goals for Alex.

LYNN: Basically, I wanted Alex to learn some of his letters so when he
     goes to kindergarten [next year] it won't be so hard and he won't be
     so frustrated. I'm not worried about his social skills. He already has
     that in him to play with other kids. He can count to 20 but he can't
     recognize the numbers. I'd like him to learn half the ABCs and the
     sounds before kindergarten. He learned how to write his first name
     and the first letter of his last name. He did learn that. Basically he
     taught his oneself how to write his name. He just looked at it and
     started to write.
ARTISHA: Like how he learned how to tie his shoes.
LYNN: He learned on his own. I was teaching him anyway, so it didn't
     matter. Whatever the preschool did was great, we were doing it
     anyway.
ARTISHA: At home, I give Alex a pen and paper and I'd take his hand
     and teach him to make an "A" and teach him the alphabets. I'd make
     boxes of stars and have him count the stars and then cut them out.
LYNN: He'd make the tally marks to count the stars instead of writing
     the numbers.
ARTISHA: I'd look in his workbook and I'd take my ideas from that.

For Lynn, while social skills are important, she is "not worried about Alex's
social skills" because he "already has that in him to play with other kids."

Like the other parents, Lynn and her family also work on literacy at home as a parallel teaching process to literacy education in preschool.

ARTISHA: Alex also has a stamp set at home.
LYNN: It has stamps, markers, pencils. Alex stamps his name all over his arms.
ARTISHA: He'll take a marker and start writing his name. He'll say, "Is this right?"
LYNN: He wants to write the baby's name, Artisha's name, my name.
ARTISHA: He also reads at home. He wants to read bedtime stories. Alex loves this book about a girl who brings honey to her auntie. It was my favorite book to read, too.

As in Regina's and Aida's families, Lynn and Artisha work together as a family to strengthen Alex's beginning literacy skills. Given Artisha's important role in teaching Alex, Artisha (like Chatani and Brianna in Regina's family and Areli in Aida's) is an older sibling who can provide her own form of developmentally appropriate and responsive teaching for Alex.

Development and Diversity

I asked Bonita for her thoughts on ways to involve diverse learners in playful and responsive literacy activities.

In a diverse classroom, this is where different centers come in. If you've got a group of kids, through trial and error figure out where they are. You can vary in small groups and use call-and-response. Stories involve kids and they like songs. They can talk and yell back. If kids get involved, their minds are going and they just blurt it out. I touch and feel and do it to understand. Akilah likes to sit back and interacts only if she feels comfortable. We all assume if one person from an ethnic group does something, then they all are, but it isn't always so.

Bonita values "call-and-response" and getting children "involved" in stories as active ways for promoting literacy with diverse learners. Noting that Akilah "likes to sit back and interacts only if she feels comfortable," Bonita points out that individual differences are important, though they may not always be tied to the traditions of an ethnic group ("We all assume if one person from an ethnic group does something, then they all are, but it isn't always so").

I asked Regina for her thoughts on the role of language in her children's literacy learning and school success.

> Ebonics doesn't bother me too much. I don't think they should teach it in school. Heck, it's everywhere. You pick it up or you don't. It's the only thing that's ours [as African Americans]. I just wish the history books would reflect what really happened to us after we were slaves—all our inventions and contributions. I mean this for all races, too. Instead of a little section here and there, by high school and college it's a shock about the truth. As parents we get caught up making money and paying our bills, our histories get lost. Trying to fit in too much with White people, we kind of didn't hand down too much of our own past and our history. You can't go to the future if you don't know the past.

For Regina, books and language play powerful roles in either negatively perpetuating or positively transforming history and children's sense of self and identity.

> All kinds of books are important. I like to know a little bit about everybody's culture. I had a multiethnic experience when I was raised by my grandmother. I try to do the same for my kids. I like to read books by African American writers, male and female. My kids are going to live in a world that's made up of that—a rainbow of people. I want them to appreciate what they offer because those people are really the foundation of this so-called United States. The people who have sweated and died for what America is today, not the people sitting back and reaping the benefits.

Lynn agreed, pointing out that her son Alex brings his knowledge of diverse cultures into his classroom experiences.

LYNN: I just want him exposed to a variety of books. If we go to the bookstore and he sees a book on M. L. King, Alex will say, "Oh mom, we read that at school."

ARTISHA: I don't think Alex will have a problem with just being hung up on his culture. He has a lot of biracial and friends of other races.

Since Lynn wants Alex to expand his language learning, she plans to enroll him in a Spanish immersion program for kindergarten.

I want him to learn a second language in kindergarten because today it seems like you need at least two languages. It makes it easier when you get out of high school. We have a growing Latino population in California, and it seems like you should know Spanish now. I also want Alex to be familiar with other cultures in addition to African American culture.

Having provided Alex with multiracial experiences outside of school, Lynn looks to school as a place to expand her son's multiethnic and multilingual learning.

I asked Aida about Spanish and English language use in home and school.

AIDA: English is OK in preschool. I speak Spanish at home. Areli knows how to read and write in Spanish and I will teach Sonia. I love my language. But I prefer that they speak both. Sometimes, Sonia mixes English and Spanish. She doesn't know some words in Spanish. When my dad came to visit, Sonia mixed Spanish and English. My dad doesn't speak English! I'm working with Sonia on reading and writing in Spanish.

ARELI: Sometimes if she doesn't know how to say something in English, she says it in Spanish. Her sentences get all mixed up. We just tell her the correct way to say something.

While English as the medium of instruction in school is fine with Aida, she is determined to promote Spanish language and literacy use at home. Both Aida and her daughter Areli work with Sonia to learn new words ("We just tell her the correct way to say something") and to read and write in Spanish ("I'm working with Sonia on reading and writing in Spanish").

Alma explained how she strengthened her children's cultural and linguistic identities.

Since I'm Mexican, I really wanted to keep my background and home, and have my kids be part of it. Not to force them to love it, but at least to understand their identity. In the future, they will wonder about it. I've seen it a lot in Mexican kids. They always wonder who they are, so we need to deal with it. I'm *not* saying to give them the answer. I want them to find it out for themselves.

As Regina expressed her desire for language and identity to reinforce each other for her children, Alma also wants her children to develop a strong sense of identity as connected to their cultural and familial origins and traditions.

> I want them to *understand* Spanish; *not* just read and write. I want them to feel Hispanic. Sometimes they say they're White, and they're not. I'm really strict with this word: Hispanic. Your background is Latin American and you speak Spanish. Besides putting them into bilingual schools, I try to get them involved in church, family, friends, and *every* summer I send them to Mexico so they can really get involved in culture.

Alma is a strong advocate for her children to self-identify as "Hispanic" and to "involve" them in Spanish-language use in varied educational and social contexts.

> They speak it [Spanish] and read it and write it. They understand. But every time they have the opportunity, they avoid it. They do. I'm kind of disappointed. I'm really the only one they speak Spanish with, and on vacation in Mexico they speak with their grandma. We live in the U.S.A. That's the bottom line. The environment most of the time is English.

Although lamenting that "every time they have the opportunity, they avoid it," Alma is determined to strengthen her children's Spanish even in the face of new legislation impeding Spanish-language teaching in California schools.

> I always have respect for the law, but [Proposition] 227 [which sought to overturn bilingual education in California] was pretty racist. I thought it was going to make things worse. I have no problem with English, but at home it gets bad. Parents can't assist their kids with homework. I know and have seen that Mexican families are really family oriented; you see a lot of kids who want to work instead of going to school. And it makes it hard. It's just because parents can't help their kids with their education. So I think that bilingual education is important. With my oldest daughter, I said I wanted a bilingual program, and they said she speaks English only. I said she's Hispanic, and I want her to be in this program. So, I just went to the principal and I said, "You're discriminating against me." And she said, "OK, your child can be in the school."

For parents who "can't help their kids with their education" and can't speak the dominant language of the school, this tears into the fabric of the family and parents' efforts to stay close to their children.

What can we do with this knowledge of parental perspectives on schooling and literacy education? The parents' perspectives on development, literacy, and diversity point to several valuable tenets for school success for children and their families.

Help children develop a strong sense of self and independence in school literacy. (Bonita: "I liked the bookbag program because it gave the kids a sense of independence, and Akilah felt proud to have her own book come home. She took care of it, and she wanted to read it as soon as she got home. She wanted to read *her* book").

Recognize the respect that parents afford teachers and parents' interest in their children's happiness. (Alma: "I think that in preschool this doesn't really matter. I don't think a three- and four-year-old cares about it. I really want the kids to really enjoy what they were doing—whatever the teacher was doing that day, whatever the subject, I was really grateful").

Coordinate preschool literacy learning with kindergarten goals and practices. (Rochelle: "Doing writing letters and tracing *shouldn't* be mandatory [in preschool] because they're going to learn it in kindergarten anyway. Some things they should learn, but if they learn everything they'll be bored [in kindergarten]. So make it in the middle, a medium, if kids know how to write their names, they can write it over and over and over again. For those who don't, they can learn it").

Recognize and incorporate parental expectations for kindergarten literacy. (Lynn: "I wanted Alex to learn some of his letters so when he goes to kindergarten [next year] it won't be so hard and he won't be so frustrated. I'm not worried about his social skills. He already has that in him to play with other kids").

Recognize and build upon the literacy teaching of entire families. (Regina: "In terms of books, Ryen loves to be read to. He memorizes. He can't read it, but he knows what it says." Ryen "reads to" his sister Brianna, and "if he knows it himself, he says it. If he doesn't, I tell him." Ryen's other sister, Chatani, likes to "point at the pictures and read to Ryen. If I say, what's in the picture? He tells me").

Learn about the variety of child-created literacy practices invented in children's homes and communities. (Aida: "At home, Sonia puts all her stuffed animals on the floor and reads to them with the book from the bookbag program. She likes to be the teacher. Sometimes she asks us to read the story").

The parents are interested in learning more about literacy education in schools and are committed advocates for their children's school success. They want to see both developmentally appropriate and culturally responsive literacy teaching going on at their children's schools. These parents, who themselves represent a diversity of backgrounds and interests, base this expectation and desire on their own educational, political, and cultural traditions and histories. They want an expanded and vibrant future for their children, and see developmentally appropriate and responsive literacy education as playing a central role in challenging and educating their children to a high level of personal and educational achievement. The parents see, too, that the literacy journeys of their children are linked in part to their own developmental journeys as parents. Parents learn alongside their children, adjusting their views on appropriate literacy education and their own goals and expectations for the socialization and upbringing of their children.

It is valuable, then, to make room in literacy theory and practice for the perspectives and views of parents. By listening to parents and learning how and why they talk about literacy for their children and for themselves, we can move closer together as teachers, children, and families. This does not mean that the home is to be changed or brought closer to the ways of school, weakening family ties and cultural traditions (Valdés, 1996). Rather, the voices of teachers and families can come together in some middle area, where local literacy expectations can meet local literacy teaching practices, making literacy education responsive to the daily and the enduring wishes and needs of children and adults.

Epilogue

I listened in on a group of children smelling their magic markers as they worked in their journals.

TYRIQUE: It smells like Altoids. You put Altoids in your mouth and it makes your breath smell good.
ARTHUR: Smell this one. It smells like bubble gum.
FRANK: It smells like BBQ Chicken McNuggets.
SHANA: That one smells like candy. It smells good.
EMILE: That's bubble gum.
RONNIE: Hmmm. (smelling) This is bubble gum. (giggles)
EMILE: I'm making my brother's room.
RONNIE: I'm makin' cartoons.
EMILE: Yeah.
RONNIE: You wanna smell this brown?
EMILE: I gots a sister. You gots a sister?
RONNIE: Yes.
EMILE: Could I see some of that blue?
RONNIE: Smell this. Smell this. Mmm. This smell good. You wanna smell this? Wanna smell this?

I have written this book as a portrait of connections between developmentally appropriate and responsive literacy education. While I used these terms throughout the book to focus attention on finding common ground in theory and practice between these frameworks, the children and the adults in this book rarely use this terminology. What do children, teachers, and parents talk about when they talk about literacy learning in school?

Markers smell and so children make physical connections to literacy (Frank: "It smells like BBQ Chicken McNuggets"). These are part of the roots of literacy—literacy as physical, literacy as action, and literacy as power. The children also create and recreate genres as they transform literacy forms and functions (Ronnie: "I'm makin' cartoons"). Children talk and interact as they do literacy to gain a greater sense of addressivity with each other and their texts (Ronnie: "You wanna smell this brown?"). Personal experiences are exchanged to strengthen family and community ties (Emile: "I gots a sister. You gots a sister?").

Teachers talk about teaching literacy based on their personal and cultural beliefs and identities (denise: "I teach from my passion, and so the community that I teach to is able to share in my story," and Pandora: "Just surrounding kids with books and assuming they will magically learn how to read. This is *not* how I learned to read"). Teachers also talk about linking literacy with performance to make books more responsive to children (Robin: "When there's something exciting in the book, change the intonation in your voice, show in your face that you're excited. Whisper the voice, yell the voice"). Teachers also talk about breaking literacy and teaching down into manageable parts for children's developmental and responsive learning (Connie: "But you then have to *break it down* to what's developmentally appropriate for *that* child").

Parents talk about their efforts to learn about their children's literacy and to explore their own developmental paths as parents (Bonita: "Was I realistic? Was she supposed to be able to read [in preschool]? In order not to be stressed out, like saying to Akilah, 'How come you can't read that?' I went back and did some research"). Parents talk about the value of attention to literacy forms and skills to provide a solid academic foundation during their children's early school years (Rochelle: "I wanted all my kids to learn all the alphabet, at least the uppercase and lowercase. . . . In kindergarten, they learn how to write their name properly. So at least they can recognize the letters of their name [in preschool]"). Parents and their families talk about collaborating on literacy together to solidify family ties and improve the literacy learning of their youngest members (Ten-year-old Areli: "Sometimes I read out of a chapter book or a picture book, and after I read, we ask Sonia [preschooler] what happened. She does good. I learned from my mom because she did this with me. I also learned from my class at school because of book reports").

So the words and perspectives of the children and adults are more varied and far richer than lists of developmentally appropriate practices or simplified guidelines for responsive teaching. I have learned that cultivating layers of literacy and layers of community in schools takes time and collaboration. There are no easy paths and no ready-made programs or quick interventions. It's not like putting up a pop-up tent. Literacy education for children and adults in today's urban schools is far messier, much more deeply tied to particular social and cultural experiences and expectations and to impassioned teaching and parenting by individual teachers and parents. But this is not to say that visions for literacy education can't be united around large patches of common ground. I hope that I have provided enough telling vignettes and perspectives for readers to see new bridges across developmental and responsive literacy theory and practice.

First, we need continued portraits of children at work and play with literacy in varied educational settings. Teacher research is one powerful way to collect these literacy stories and portraits. As we hear and see more of children's words and thoughts, we can gain a more complicated picture of where children are, what they can do, and where they want to go. The variety of ways that the children in this book approach dictation, read books, and share out-of-school experiences indicates the power of diverse and yet inclusive portraits of children's literacy learning.

Second, it is valuable to see children's own literacy efforts as reflective of their developmental capabilities and their potential for responsiveness to each other and to texts. In these instances of self-scaffolding and peer–peer assistance, the children provide themselves and each other with developmentally appropriate and responsive teaching to further their literacy competency and social inclusion. In seeing and documenting the children's own efforts, we can shift some of the practical work of literacy education away from teachers and parents and toward children's developing abilities to teach and learn with and from each other. And by looking at the strategies that children use to get into and sustain their book reading, such as starting off and in-text strategies, we can further broaden our view of what children can do to promote their own literacy development.

Third, it is important to take a long view of children's language arts and literacy learning. This means that teachers and parents need to link hands across such professional dividing lines as preschool and elementary school, and to link these arenas of learning more recursively. In this way, children do not make a transition from preschool to kindergarten, but rather follow a dynamic, back-and-forth journey as preschool and kindergarten literacy are connected in theory and practice. This means that preschool and kindergarten teachers need to talk to each other, and literacy frameworks need to incorporate this dynamic nature of children's literacy learning.

Fourth, it is valuable to hear the perspectives of teachers on possible common ground between developmentally appropriate and responsive literacy teaching. Hearing their experiences and views helps particularize these frameworks, grounding them in local situations and particular contexts. From this we can see what is applicable and worth keeping, and what is not. Literacy theory and practice are tested in the daily lives of teachers and children in classrooms. The voices of teachers make their imprint on the lists and guidelines for effective literacy education by personalizing the general and leading children in the moment-to-moment decisions of literacy education. In this way, the big nets of developmentally appropriate and responsive teaching strategies and goals are brought closer to home, closer to children and adults. Listening to teachers also helps us see literacy teaching as an art, a creative endeavor that changes and evolves over time. Teachers, like children, also have their own developmental paths for teaching literacy in new ways.

Fifth, it is essential to expand the theoretical and practical circles of literacy education to include the voices of parents and families. Like teachers, parents experience their own developmental journeys as individuals and as parents. In this way, they also are learning to advocate for their children's literacy and academic success in schools. Parents are learning how to navigate the school system, learning about the literacy ways of school, and all the while holding fast to their literacy expectations and practices from home and community. Parents are their children's teachers at home, instructing them in certain basic literacy skills and allowing children the freedom to structure their own literacy strategies and activities. In strengthening the connections between home and school, and *not* asking children and parents to choose one over the other, the perspectives and needs of families can influence the direction and tenor of children's school literacy learning.

When I started to write this book, I thought about common ground between developmentally appropriate and responsive literacy education. I asked myself how I could connect these two ideas to help children learn literacy. I have now ended up back at the beginning, thinking about what four-year-old Kyesha meant when she said, "Oooh girl, you're scribble scrabbling! You oughta be ashamed of yourself!" and what Robin meant when he told me, "whisper the voice, yell the voice," when reading with children. These are really the details of literacy that we remember as children and adults, for these are the human and personal details of literacy and growing up in schools and communities. Children and adults alike want to "get bigger" and "get smarter." It is my hope that readers will remember these details, spin them out and let them touch and come closer to the instances of literacy education in other settings and with other children and adults. I hope, too, that more connections are made, and new potentials for common ground are seen through other drawings of "bald headed Michael Jordans dunking over Shaq" and conversations about "Marine World is gonna be bad" and "the last time I went to Marine World with my granny, I saw an elephant."

At the end of a recent puppet show at Hawthorne Preschool, the puppeteer asked the children if they had any questions. Marvin raised his hand and asked, "Can you show us the mess?" The puppeteer looked puzzled.

"He means," I said, "that he wants to see what's behind the puppet stage." Marvin remembered that a previous puppeteer had dismantled his stage to show the children how the puppets move and how he manipulated the props. Marvin was delighted with this behind-the-scenes look into the puppet show, and so he asked to see the "mess." Later on, I thought back to Marvin's smile and delight as the second puppeteer also dismantled the stage and showed us how he did his show. The stage was different, and so were the props and puppets. This is what I want my literacy teaching to be about for children—to show them the "mess" and the inner workings of their words and books and drawings. I want them to hear the sound of their words and symbols, and see the intentions and movements lying underneath and behind. "Can you show us the mess?" Marvin was right on track, close to what made excellent developmental and responsive sense to children. Marvin slapped his thighs and half-jumped out of his seat as the puppeteer raised one puppet after another, moving their arms and their legs and recreating their voices and characters.

Children's Literature

Aagard, J. (1989). *The calypso alphabet*. New York: Henry Holt.

Asch, F. (1982). *Happy birthday, moon*. New York: Scholastic.

Bang, M. (1983). *Ten, nine, eight*. New York: Scholastic.

Barton, B. (1989). *Dinosaurs, dinosaurs*. New York: HarperCollins.

Brett, J. (1989). *The mitten*. New York: Putnam's.

Carle, E. (1969). *The very hungry caterpillar*. New York: Philomel.

Carle, E. (1990). *The very quiet cricket*. New York: Philomel.

Crews, N. (1995). *One hot summer day*. New York: Greenwillow Books.

Cummings, P. (1991). *Clean up your room, Harvey Moon!* New York: Simon & Schuster.

Ehlert, L. (1992). *Fish eyes*. New York: Harcourt Brace.

Ehlert, L. (1992). *Moon rope/Un lazo a la luna*. New York: Harcourt Brace.

Ehlert, L. (1995). *Snowballs*. New York: Harcourt Brace.

Emberley, E. (1993). *Go away, big green monster!* Boston: Little Brown.

Feder, J. (1995). *Table, chair, bear: A book in many languages*. New York: Ticknor & Fields.

Fleming, D. (1992). *Count!* New York: Henry Holt.

French, V. (1994). *Red Hen and Sly Fox*. New York: Simon & Schuster.

Hill, E. (1993). *Spot pasea por el bosque*. New York: Putnam.

Hoban, T. (1987). *26 letters and 99 cents*. New York: Greenwillow Books.

Kalan, R. (1981). *Jump, frog, jump/¡Salta, ranita, salta!* New York: Mulberry Books.

Keller, H. (1992). *Island baby*. New York: Morrow.

Lobel, A. (1970). *Frog and toad are friends*. New York: HarperCollins.

Macquitty, M. (1992). *Sharks: Eyewitness books*. New York: Knopf.

Martin, B., & Archambault, J. (1989). *Chicka chicka boom boom*. New York: Simon & Schuster.

Martin, B., & Carle, E. (1967). *Brown bear, brown bear, what do you see?* New York: Holt, Rinehart and Winston.

Matero, R. (1994). *Reptiles*. Chicago: Kidsbooks.

McDermott, G. (1972). *Anansi the spider*. New York: Holt, Rinehart and Winston.

McDermott, G. (1992). *Zomo the rabbit*. New York: Harcourt Brace.

Pinkney, A., & Pinkney, B. (1997). *Pretty brown face*. New York: Harcourt Brace.

Raschka, C. (1993). *Yo! yes!* New York: Orchard Books.

Rosen, M., & Oxenbury, H. (1989). *We're going on a bear hunt*. New York: Margaret K. McElderry Books.

Sardegna, J. (1994). *K is for kiss goodnight*. New York: Bantam Doubleday.

Smalls, I. (1992). *Jonathan and his mommy.* Boston: Little, Brown.

Smith, J., & Parkes, B. (1986). *The three billy goats gruff.* London: Tadpole Books.

Soto, G. (1996). *The old man & his door.* New York: Putnam's.

Steptoe, J. (Illustrator). (1997). *In daddy's arms I am tall: African Americans celebrating fathers.* New York: Lee & Low Books.

Strickland, P., & Strickland, H. (1994). *Dinosaur roar!* New York: Scholastic.

Understanding opposites. (1996). New York: Dutton Books.

Wild, M. (1987). *There's a sea in my bedroom.* St. Petersburg, FL: Willowisp.

Wildsmith, B. (1965). *Brian Wildsmith's 1, 2, 3's.* Oxford: Oxford University Press.

Wildsmith, B. (1982). *Cat on the mat.* Oxford: Oxford University Press.

Wildsmith. B. (1983). *The apple bird.* Oxford: Oxford University Press.

Wood, A. (1982). *Quick as a cricket.* Clarkston, MI: Child's Play.

Young, E. (1989). *Lon Po Po: A Red-Riding Hood story from China.* New York: Scholastic.

Zemach, M. (1983). *The little red hen: An old story.* Toronto: Collins.

References

Ada, A. F. (1988). The Pajaro Valley experience: Working with Spanish-speaking parents to develop children's reading and writing skills in the home through the use of children's literature. In T. Skutnabb-Kangas & J. Cummins (Eds.), *Minority education—From shame to struggle* (pp. 223–238). Philadelphia: Multi-Lingual Matters.

Ashton-Warner, S. (1963). *Teacher*. London: Virago.

Au, K. H., & Jordan, C. (1981). Teaching reading to Hawaiian children: Finding a culturally appropriate solution. In H. Trueba, G. P. Guthrie, & K. H. Au (Eds.), *Culture in the bilingual classroom: Studies in classroom ethnography* (pp. 139–152). Rowley, MA: Newbury House.

Bakhtin, M. M. (1981). *The dialogic imagination: Four essays by M. M. Bakhtin* (M. Holquist, Ed.; C. Emerson & M. Holquist, Trans.). Austin: University of Texas Press.

Bakhtin, M. M. (1986). *Speech genres & other late essays* (C. Emerson & M. Holquist, Eds.; V. W. McGee, Trans.). Austin: University of Texas Press.

Bishop, R. S. (1990). Walk tall in the world: African American literature for today's children. *Journal of Negro Education, 59*(4), 556–565.

Bissex, G. (1980). *Gnys at wrk: A child learns to read and write*. Cambridge, MA: Harvard University Press.

Bissex, G., & Bullock, R. (1987). *Seeing for ourselves: Case study research by teachers of writing*. Portsmouth, NH: Heinemann.

Bloch, M. (1991). Critical science and history of child development's influence on the aims and effects of early education. *Early Education and Development, 2*(2), 95–108.

Bogdan, R. C., & Biklen, S. K. (1998). *Qualitative research in education: An introduction to theory and practice* (3rd ed.). Boston: Allyn & Bacon.

Bredekamp, S., & Copple, C. (Eds.). (1997). *Developmentally appropriate practice in early childhood programs* (rev. ed.). Washington, DC: National Association for the Education of Young Children.

Britsch, S. (1994). The contribution of the preschool to a Native American community. In A. H. Dyson & C. Genishi (Eds.), *The need for story: Cultural diversity in classroom and community* (pp. 199–205). Urbana, IL: National Council of Teachers of English.

Britton, J. (1983). Writing and the story world. In B. M. Kroll & G. Wells (Eds.), *Explorations in the development of writing* (pp. 3–30). London: Wiley.

Bruner, J. (1986). *Actual minds, possible worlds*. Cambridge, MA: Harvard University Press.

Bruner, J. (1994). Life as narrative. In A. H. Dyson & C. Genishi (Eds.), *The need for story: Cultural diversity in classroom and community* (pp. 28–37). Urbana, IL: National Council of Teachers of English.

Bruner, J. (1996). *The culture of education.* Cambridge, MA: Harvard University Press.

Cadwell, L. B. (1997). *Bringing Reggio Emilia home: An innovative approach to early childhood education.* New York: Teachers College Press.

Cazden, C. (1982). Contexts for literacy: In the mind and in the classroom. *Journal of Reading Behavior, 14,* 413–427.

Clay, M. (1975). *What did I write?* Portsmouth, NH: Heinemann.

Cochran-Smith, M., & Lytle, S. (1993). *Inside/outside—Teacher research and knowledge.* New York: Teachers College Press.

Coles, R. (1989). *The call of stories: Teaching and the moral imagination.* Boston: Houghton Mifflin.

Corsaro, W. (1985). *Friendship and peer culture in the early years.* Norwood, NJ: Ablex.

Continuity for young children: Positive transitions to elementary school. (1997). Sacramento: California Department of Education.

Cummins, J. (1986). Empowering minority students: A framework for intervention. *Harvard Educational Review, 56*(1), 18–36.

Delgado-Gaitan, C. (1996). *Protean literacy: Extending the discourse on empowerment.* London: Falmer Press.

Delpit, L. (1995). *Other people's children: Cultural conflict in the classroom.* New York: Free Press.

Donaldson, M. (1978). *Children's minds.* New York: Norton.

Dyson, A. H. (1986). Appreciate the drawing and dictating of young children. *Young Children, 43*(3), 379–409.

Dyson, A. H. (1993). *Social worlds of children learning to write in an urban primary school.* New York: Teachers College Press.

Dyson, A. H. (1997). *Writing superheroes: Contemporary childhood, popular culture, and classroom literacy.* New York: Teachers College Press.

Edwards, C., Gandini, L., & Forman, G. (Eds.). (1998). *The hundred languages of children: The Reggio Emilia approach to early childhood education* (2nd ed.). Norwood, NJ: Ablex.

Elkind, D. (1981). *The hurried child.* Reading, MA: Addison-Wesley.

Erickson, F. (1986). Qualitative methods in research on teaching. In M. C. Wittrock (Ed.), *Handbook of research on teaching* (3rd ed.; pp. 119–161). New York: Macmillan.

Every child a reader: The report of the California reading task force. (1995). Sacramento: California Department of Education.

Ferreiro, E., & Teberosky, A. (1982). *Literacy before schooling.* Exeter, NH: Heinemann.

Fillmore, L. W. (1979). Individual differences in second language acquisition. In C. J. Fillmore, D. Kempler, & W. S-Y. Wang (Eds.), *Individual differences in language ability and language behavior* (pp. 203–228). New York: Academic Press.

Gadsden, V. (1994). Understanding family literacy: Conceptual issues facing the field. *Teachers College Record, 96*(1), 78–89.

Gates, H. L., III. (1988). *The signifying monkey: A theory of Afro-American literary criticism.* New York: Oxford University Press.

Genishi, C. (1982). Observational research methods for early childhood education. In B. Spodek (Ed.), *Handbook of research in early childhood education* (pp. 516–537). New York: Free Press.

Goodwin, W. L., & Goodwin, L. D. (1996*). Understanding quantitative and qualitative research in early childhood education.* New York: Teachers College Press.

Goswami, D., & Stillman, P. R. (Eds.). (1987). *Reclaiming the classroom: Teacher research as an agency for change.* Portsmouth, NH: Heinemann.

Graves, D. (1983). *Writing: Teachers & children at work.* Portsmouth, NH: Heinemann.

Gutierrez, K., & Larson, J. (1994). Language borders: Recitation as hegemonic discourse. *International Journal of Educational Reform, 3*(1), 22–36.

Harris, V. J. (1990). African American children's literature: The first one hundred years. *Journal of Negro Education, 59*(4), 540–555.

Hatch, E. (1992). *Discourse and language education.* Cambridge: Cambridge University Press.

Heath, S. B. (1983). *Ways with words.* Cambridge: Cambridge University Press.

Hicks, D. (1998). Narrative discourse as inner and outer word. *Language Arts, 75*(1), 28–34.

hooks, b. (1994). *Teaching to transgress: Education as the practice of freedom.* New York: Routledge.

Hymes, D. (1972). Introduction. In C. Cazden, V. P. John, & D. Hymes (Eds.), *Functions of language in the classroom* (pp. xi–lvii). New York: Teachers College Press.

Igoa, C. (1995). *The inner world of the immigrant child.* New York: St. Martin's Press.

Jipson, J. (1991). Developmentally appropriate practice: Culture, curriculum, connections. *Early Education and Development, 2*(2), 120–136.

King, M. L., & Rentel, V. M. (1981). *How children learn to write: A longitudinal study.* Columbus: Ohio State University.

Ladson-Billings, G. (1994). *The dreamkeepers: Successful teachers of African American children.* San Francisco: Jossey-Bass.

Ladson-Billings, G. (1998). [Interview with A. I. Willis & K. C. Lewis]. *Language Arts, 75*(1), 61–70.

Learning to read and write: Developmentally appropriate practices for young children. (1998). (Joint position statement of the International Reading Association and the National Association for the Education of Young Children). *Young Children, 53*(4), 30–46.

Lee, C. D. (1991). Big picture talkers/words walking without masters: The instructional implications for ethnic voices for an expanded literacy. *Journal of Negro Education, 60*(3), 291–304.

Levin, D. (1998). *Remote control childhood? Combating the hazards of media culture.* Washington, DC: National Association for the Education of Young Children.

Lubeck, S. (1998). Is developmentally appropriate practice for everyone? *Childhood Education, 74*(5), 283–292.

Mallory, B. L., & New, R. S. (Eds.). (1994). *Diversity and developmentally appropriate practices: Challenges for early childhood education.* New York: Teachers College Press.

McNamee, G. D. (1987). The social origins of narrative skills. In M. Hickman (Ed.), *Social and functional approaches to language and thought* (pp. 287–304). New York: Academic Press.

Meier, D. R. (1997). *Learning in small moments: Life in an urban classroom.* New York: Teachers College Press.

Moll, L. C., Amanti, C., Neff, D., & Gonzalez, N. (1992). Funds of knowledge for teaching: Using a qualitative approach to connect homes and classrooms. *Theory Into Practice, 31*(2), 132–141.

Montessori, M. (1995). *The absorbent mind.* New York: Henry Holt.

Moore, R. (1998). *Investigating culturally engaged instruction: A report to the Spencer Foundation.* Chicago: Spencer Foundation.

National Research Council. (1998). *Preventing reading difficulties in young children.* National Academy Press.

New, R. (1994). Culture, child development, and developmentally appropriate practices. In B. L. Mallory & R. S. New (Eds.), *Diversity and developmentally appropriate practices: Challenges for early childhood education* (pp. 65–83). New York: Teachers College Press.

New, R. (1999). An integrated early childhood curriculum: Moving from the what to the how to the why. In C. Seefeldt (Ed.), *The early childhood curriculum: Current findings in theory and practice* (3rd ed.; pp. 265–287). New York: Teachers College Press.

New, R. S., & Mallory, B. L. (1994). Introduction: The ethic of inclusion. In B. L. Mallory & R. S. New (Eds.), *Diversity and developmentally appropriate practices: Challenges for early childhood education* (pp. 1–16). New York: Teachers College Press.

Ochs, E. J. (1988). *Culture and language development.* Cambridge: Cambridge University Press.

Paley, V. G. (1981). *Wally's stories.* Cambridge, MA: Harvard University Press.

Piaget, J. (1952). *The origins of intelligence in children.* New York: International Universities Press.

Rosen, H. (1977, April). *The nurture of narrative.* Paper presented at the annual meeting of the International Reading Association, Chicago.

Scribner, S., & Cole, M. (1981). *The psychology of literacy.* Cambridge, MA: Harvard University Press.

Stremmel, A. J. (1997). Diversity and the multicultural perspective. In C. H. Hart, D. C. Burts, & R. Charlesworth (Eds.), *Integrated curriculum and developmentally appropriate practice: Birth to age eight* (pp. 363–388). Albany: State University of New York Press.

Sulzby, E. (1985). Kindergartners as writers and readers. In M. Farr (Ed.), *Advances in writing research: Vol. 1. Children's early writing development* (pp. 127–199). Norwood, NJ: Ablex.

Sulzby, E. (1987). Children's development of prosodic distinctions in telling and dication modes. In A. Matsuhashi (Ed.), *Writing in real time: Modelling production processes* (pp. 133–160). Norwood, NJ: Ablex.

Tabors, P. (1997). *One child, two languages: A guide for preschool educators of children learning English as a second language.* Baltimore: Paul H. Brooks.

Taylor, D. (1997). *Many families, many literacies: An international declaration of principles.* Portsmouth, NH: Heinemann.

Teaching reading: A balanced, comprehensive approach to teaching reading in prekindergarten through grade three. (1996). Sacramento: California Department of Education.

The unique power of reading and how to unleash it. (1998, Spring/Summer). *American Educator, 22* (1, 2).

Valdés, G. (1996). *Con respeto: Bridging the distances between culturally diverse families and schools.* New York: Teachers College Press.

Vygotsky, L. S. (1978). *Mind in society.* Cambridge, MA: Harvard University Press.

Vygotsky, L. S. (1986). *Thought and language.* Cambridge, MA: MIT Press.

Wertsch, J. (1980). The significance of dialogue in Vygotsky's account of social, egocentric, and inner speech. *Contemporary Educational Psychology, 5,* 150–162.

Wertsch, J. (1991). *Voices of the mind: A sociocultural approach to mediated action.* Cambridge, MA: Harvard University Press.

Willis, A. I. (1995). Reading the world of school literacy: Contextualizing the experience of a young African American male. *Harvard Educational Review, 65*(1), 30–49.

Index

About the Author

Daniel Meier teaches courses in language, literacy, and early childhood education in the Department of Elementary Education at San Francisco State University. He holds degrees from Wesleyan University, Harvard University, and the University of California at Berkeley. The author of articles on literacy and early childhood education, Meier is also the author of *Learning in Small Moments: Life in an Urban Classroom* (Teachers College Press, 1997). He has taught kindergarten and first grade in both private and public elementary schools, and currently teaches part-time in urban preschools in the San Francisco Bay Area, working with teachers, children, and families on language and literacy development. He lives with his wife Hazelle and daughter Kaili in the San Francisco Bay Area. The author invites correspondence to: Daniel Meier, Department of Elementary Education, San Francisco State University, 1600 Holloway Avenue, San Francisco, CA 94132. Electronic mail: *dmeier@sfsu.edu*